Economic Prosperity Recaptured

CESifo Book Series
Hans-Werner Sinn, editor

Economic Prosperity Recaptured

The Finnish Path from Crisis to Rapid Growth

Seppo Honkapohja, Erkki A. Koskela, Willi Leibfritz, and Roope Uusitalo

CESifo Book Series

The MIT Press
Cambridge, Massachusetts
London, England

For information about special quantity discounts, please e-mail special_sales@mitpress.mit.edu

This book was set in Palatino on 3B2 by Asco Typesetters, Hong Kong.
Printed and bound in the United States of America.

Library of Congress Cataloging-in-Publication Data

Economic prosperity recaptured : the Finnish path from crisis to rapid growth / Seppo Honkapohja ... [et al.].
  p. cm. — (CESifo book series)
Includes bibliographical references and index.
ISBN 978-0-262-01269-0 (hardcover : alk. paper)
1. Finland—Economic conditions—1981– 2. Finland—Economic policy. I. Honkapohja, Seppo, 1951–
HC340.2.E26   2009
330.94897'034—dc22   2008041709

10 9 8 7 6 5 4 3 2 1

Contents

CESifo Book Series Foreword

This volume is part of the CESifo Book Series. Each book in the series aims to cover a topical policy issue in economics. The monographs reflect the research agenda of the Ifo Institute for Economic Research and they are typically "tandem projects" where internationally renowned economists from the CESifo network cooperate with Ifo researchers. The monographs have been anonymously refereed and revised after being presented and discussed at several workshops hosted by the Ifo Institute.

Preface

Many countries have experienced major economic changes in the period since the mid-1980s as a result of liberalization and deregulation—the two key aspects of the ongoing processes of globalization. For individual countries, the formulation and conduct of economic policies have played a major role in the ups and downs of the national economies during the resulting adjustment processes. Many countries have gone through periods of crisis and success as a result of both bad and good economic policies. In this book we focus on the case of Finland, a small country of some five million people. In recent years, Finland has been hailed as a great success story and as a role model for other countries.

The story of Finland is in fact quite complex and provides an excellent example of both successful and unsuccessful economic policies in response to changing circumstances. Deregulation of the financial system and macroeconomic policies have played a big part in the boom-bust cycle of the Finnish economy. We will analyze the initial periods of overheating in the second half of the 1980s and the deep crisis in the first half of the 1990s as reactions to financial deregulation, misguided economic policies, and negative international shocks. Macroeconomic policies were redirected during the crisis, which helped to turn the economy around from decline to growth. Since the mid-1990s economic growth has been quite rapid. This has to a large extent resulted from a rapid structural transformation of Finland into a high tech economy. Business skills and luck have played key roles in the transformation, but well-designed economic policies have also contributed to the success story of Finland since the mid-1990s.

This book is aimed at a wider audience than just those with a special interest in Finland. We compare experiences of Finland to those of other countries at various stages of the analysis. In this way we hope the book will provide some useful lessons regarding economic management and policies for other countries amidst the processes of globalization.

This book has its origins in a study of the Finnish crisis by Seppo Honkapohja and Erkki Koskela, which appeared in *Economic Policy* in 1999. That study has been updated and expanded in various directions, especially as regards the period of rapid growth since the mid-1990s and through more extensive international comparisons. The two other authors, Willi Leibfritz and Roope Uusitalo, have made major contributions in particular to these parts of the book.

The book has to a significant extent been written in the Research Unit on Economic Structures and Growth (RUESG) at the University of Helsinki, directed jointly by Honkapohja and Koskela until 2004 and by Koskela thereafter. Honkapohja acknowledges the hospitality of RUESG from 2004 onward after his move first to the University of Cambridge and then to the Bank of Finland at the beginning of 2008. The views expressed in the book are those of the authors and not of the Bank of Finland.

A large number of people have offered useful comments on the different versions of the book manuscript. We want to thank especially Jukka Jalava, Jaakko Kiander, Jorma Ollila, Matti Pohjola, Hans-Werner Sinn, Khaled Soufani, Pentti Vartia, Vesa Vihriälä, and anonymous referees. We are also grateful to a number of people who have provided research assistance in the project: Manu Heikkonen, Janne Hukka, Juhana Hukkinen, Esa Jokivuolle, Heikki Kauppi, Markku Lanne, Hanna-Leena Männistö, Juho Ullakonoja, Janne Villanen, and Tarja Yrjölä. We also thank Glenn Harma for checking the English. The book has been presented in two CESifo seminars, in November 2003 and January 2005; in a seminar at the Bank of Finland in June 2005; in the meeting of the Finnish Academy of Science and Letters in February 2006; and in a seminar in the University of Oulu in April 2006. The audiences in these events provided us with useful comments and questions. Finally, we wish to thank CESifo for taking an active interest in the project.

1   Introduction

The period since the late 1980s is seen in economic history as a time of major changes in both the European and world economies. There have been several notable developments. The breakdown of socialism in Eastern and East-Central Europe was a dramatic event in the European political landscape. It also initiated major structural changes in Europe. The most significant changes naturally occurred within the former socialist countries themselves, but the neighboring countries were also affected.

Economic integration in the European Union (EU) deepened with the creation of the single-market program. EU enlargements were important events for Europe. First, three EFTA/EEA countries (Austria, Finland and Sweden) sought close integration with the European Union and became members in 1995. The second expansion occurred in May 2004 when ten new members joined the European Union, including eight East-Central European and two Mediterranean countries. Clearly, the latter development entailed a major change and its effects are only now beginning to be realized across the whole EU arena. As is well known, further EU expansion is underway. Bulgaria and Romania joined the EU in the beginning of 2008, and later Croatia and possibly Turkey, are likely to become members of the European Union in the coming years.

In the world economy the general tendencies of liberalization and deregulation, often called "globalization," have been a major economic force since the late 1980s. It is important to focus on the liberalization and deregulation of national financial systems, which have had major macroeconomic effects in several countries, including some strong performers in East Asia as well as some countries in Latin America. After opening their markets and financial systems to international forces, these countries experienced financial crises that led to traumatic short-run economic fluctuations but that in the longer term facilitated structural change.

Financial crises also occurred in some European countries, including Finland, Sweden, and Norway. In Europe, monetary integration has been at the core of the EU single-market program. The liberalization of capital movements in the second half of the 1980s caused problems for the European monetary system, and its regime of fixed exchange rates (ERM) encountered several currency crises in the early 1990s. These were eventually overcome and the Economic and Monetary Union (EMU) was established in 1998 with a new currency, the euro. In the EMU, the European Central Bank has been in charge of the common monetary policy since the start of 1999 for the eleven original member countries, with Greece added at the beginning of 2001 as well as Slovenia in 2007.[1]

1.1 Finland in the Turbulent Times

The global economic changes in turn entailed major economic and political challenges for individual countries. These challenges were felt particularly strongly in small economies outside the economic core of Europe. An interesting case is Finland, a small country in Northern Europe with a population of just over five million people. In this book our aim is to analyze how Finland coped with the major changes in its economic environment. The Finnish economy experienced a boom in the late 1980s, following by a deep depression in the early 1990s. Finally, renewed economic growth and prosperity were achieved in the second half of the 1990s.

We will describe and analyze these three relatively distinct periods and the factors behind the rapid swings in the economy. With the benefit of hindsight we ponder whether the macroeconomic policy response to the changing external circumstances was adequate. Moreover, we will use the Finnish experience to test for real economic effects of financial constraints and look for evidence of the "credit channel" of the monetary system. We will also elaborate on the roles of the information and communication technology (ICT) revolution and economic policies in the resumption of economic growth.

As an initial illustration of the Finnish experience we look briefly at some key data. Figure 1.1 displays indexes for the level of purchasing power parity (PPP)–adjusted GDP in Finland, Sweden, and EU-15

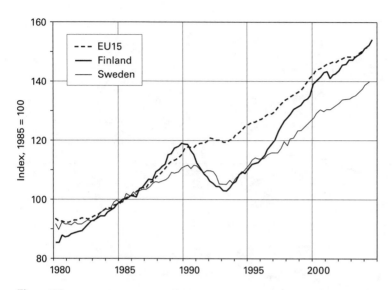

Figure 1.1
PPP-adjusted GDP for Finland, Sweden and 15 EU-countries. *Source*: Statistics Finland and Eurostat

countries.[2] The figure attests that Finland's economic experiences in the second half of the 1980s through the 1990s were indeed dramatic. For instance, compared to Finland, Sweden experienced qualitatively similar—but less pronounced—developments due to some similar and some importantly dissimilar factors, which we spell out later on. The fifteen EU countries on average experienced a standstill in growth in the early 1990s, but clearly, as figure 1.1 shows, overall economic developments in the other Western fifteen EU countries were much more benign.

As figure 1.1 indicates, the Finnish economy first experienced a strong upswing and overheating in the 1980s. At the start of the 1990s, things turned around quite rapidly and an economic crisis emerged, as indicated by a sharp drop in GDP and a rapid rise in unemployment. In the mid-1990s growth resumed and the economy began to flourish.

Developments in unemployment are shown in figure 1.2. As real GDP fell by about 14 percent from the peak in 1990 to the bottom in 1993, the rate of unemployment rose from 3 percent in 1990 to almost 20 percent at the onset of 1994. After 1994 the economy started to recover and economic growth was fairly rapid until the slowdown in the world economy in 2001. In the period 1995–2001 the average rate of

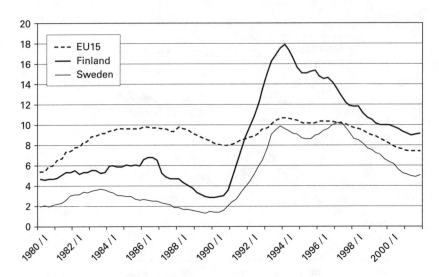

Figure 1.2
Standardized unemployment rates in Finland, Sweden and 15 EU countries. *Source*:
OECD Main Economic Indicators. Before 1988 EU-12 from OECD Employment Outlook

GDP growth was 3.3 percent per annum, which is the second highest
rate among the Western fifteen EU countries. However, despite the
rapid growth of real GDP, the decrease in the unemployment rate has
been relatively slow, and it remains at a high level of 7–8 percent.
Rapid economic growth usually helps to reduce unemployment. This
also happened in Finland, but seemingly in a relatively sluggish manner. Later, we tackle the issue of why rapid economic growth and high
unemployment have prevailed simultaneously in the Finnish case. To
repeat, figure 1.2 presents the seasonally adjusted standardized unemployment rates in Finland, Sweden, and EU-15 since 1980. The Finnish
and Swedish unemployment rates were far below the European average for most of the 1980s, but in both countries the unemployment
rates increased rapidly and displayed very similar time patterns in the
early 1990s.

These two key macroeconomic figures reflect the tip of the iceberg.
The Finnish depression of the 1990s was the most serious economic
crisis in its peacetime history. By many measures, it was more severe
than the depression of the 1930s. In fact, it is the most severe peacetime
economic crisis seen since the World War II in any of OECD economies. The 1990s crisis had many features that are not included in a
standard business cycle of the market economy. These involve the

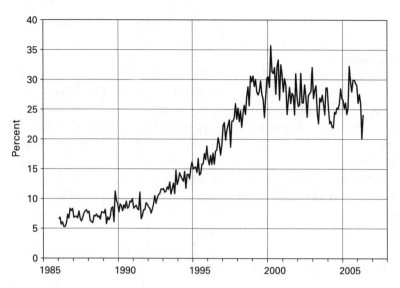

Figure 1.3
Share of high-tech exports in total exports. *Source*: National Board of Customs

huge expansion of bank lending as a consequence of financial market deregulation and major inflows of foreign capital during the boom, periods of speculative attack on the currency, relatively high real interest rates partly due to tight monetary policy, and the emergence of a major banking crisis as part of the depression.

The recovery from the economic crisis has been equally remarkable. Economic growth resumed; new firms and industries became prominent and brought affluence to Finnish society. Finland experienced a dramatic change from a traditional industrial country to a high-tech economy. Figure 1.3 shows high-tech exports as a percentage of total exports for Finland. In the ten years from 1990 to 2000 the share rose from about 7–8 percent to nearly 30 percent, which reflects the transformation to a high-technology country.

One part of the success story lies in macroeconomic policies and political developments, which provided economic predictability and stability for the Finnish economy. We will argue later that successful macroeconomic management in many (albeit not all) respects has been an important part, but of course not the entirety, of the success story of the late 1990s. We will also study structural changes in the economy favoring the high-technology sectors and argue that they played a large role in the recent Finnish miracle. In the last section of the book we attempt to look ahead to the primary future challenges of the Finnish economy and hence to the challenges facing macroeconomic management.

In brief, the story of Finland since the late 1980s and the 1990s is one of a boom-bust cycle and a miraculous recovery. The boom-bust cycle was due to major positive and negative shocks and also to the inadequate macroeconomic and other policy responses to them. The successful recovery and rapid growth since the turnaround can be attributed to better economic policy, success in the information technology revolution, and successful internationalization of the Finnish society. Despite these very positive developments, unemployment remained at a relatively high level due to both large structural changes in the economy and a lack of labor market reforms.

1.2   Lessons from Finnish Experience?

While an analysis of Finnish economic developments is clearly of some intrinsic interest due to the huge changes that took place, a major motivation for writing this book is to describe the important lessons that can be drawn from the Finnish experience. In the last twenty years Finland has experienced huge structural changes. In the first half of 1980s Finland still had a fairly tightly regulated financial system with a limited degree of competition. Traditional industries—wood and metal products—were Finland's major export industries. The past can be usefully contrasted with the present. Nowadays, Finland is a country in which a large high-technology industry and its exports play a major role. Its financial system is market-based and fairly well integrated with that of Western Europe. In this book we also consider the macroeconomic and other economic policies that Finnish policymakers carried out during this period. We argue that some policy choices turned out to be misguided, while others were relatively successful. We also analyze the underlying structural conditions that enabled Finland to achieve the remarkably rapid structural change from traditional industries to an economy with a large high-tech sector.

European integration and, more generally, globalization are clearly providing numerous new economic opportunities to many countries that are less advanced than the Western European and North American economies. However, taking advantage of these opportunities requires good macroeconomic management, and we hope that the

Finnish experience since the late 1980s can provide useful guidance in this respect. In our opinion, several other countries presently face situations and policy choices that are somewhat similar to those faced by Finnish decision makers in the late 1980s.

The financial crisis in Finland in the 1990s is one part of these similarities. Weakness in the financial system is relevant at least for some new and prospective EU member countries. Several new EU member countries are currently going through a period of fast growth and a risk of overheating that is, to a significant degree, due to big increases in inflows of foreign capital as a result of a higher degree of economic integration. Fast growth and inflows of foreign capital are creating pressures for appreciation of the currencies of these countries. The appreciation is resisted by countries that hope to join the EMU soon. Some of these countries have fairly fragile financial systems, which is another possible source of instability for the future.[3] This situation could easily lead to macroeconomic volatility in the coming years.

The challenges are not only macroeconomic. One must add that major structural changes are needed before these countries can achieve the goal of higher living standards in the future. Finland was successful in transforming itself from a traditional industrial country into a high-tech economy. We hope that the Finnish experience can highlight these challenges and thus be of some help in pointing toward appropriate policies for the coming years.

In our book we proceed as follows. The next chapter focuses on the Finnish economic crisis of the early 1990s, describing the main developments. It also contains an econometric analysis of the role of financing constraints on consumption and investment behavior. Chapter 3 continues the analysis of the Finnish crisis by looking at macroeconomic policies—monetary and exchange-rate policy and fiscal policy—before, during, and after the crisis. The chapter also considers the role of wage policy. The remaining chapters shift the focus to the upswing and rapid economic growth that took place after the early 1990s. Chapter 4 considers the resumption of economic growth and the factors behind it. Naturally, the rapid growth was partly enabled by the available unused productive capacities. However, this was not the whole story, and we analyze the major structural changes that occurred in Finland during the upswing. Chapter 5 continues the analysis of economic growth, emphasizing the importance of the Finnish educational system and human capital. Chapter 6 discusses research and development spending in Finland and takes up the emergence and current role of the New Economy in Finland by assessing the role of information and communication technologies in economic growth. The chapter also looks at the case of Nokia and the major role it played in the Finnish growth process of the 1990s. Chapter 7 concludes by summarizing Finland's policy achievements and discussing some of the current economic challenges the country faces.

2   The Crisis of the Early 1990s

In this chapter we formulate an interpretation of the Finnish economic crisis of the early 1990s. We argue that the slump in the early 1990s was no ordinary recession. Even though the Finnish economy experienced several exogenous shocks during both the boom and the bust periods, the shocks are only one part of the story. The case of Finland is a very good example of a classic financial crisis, as in Norway in the mid-1980s and Sweden in early 1990s. Financial crises have also been experienced in countries as different as Chile in the early 1980s, Mexico in the mid-1990s, and some of the East Asian countries in the late 1990s.

The Finnish case is particularly interesting because the economy achieved a remarkable recovery from the crisis, with a turnaround in 1994 and subsequent rapid real growth. This chapter focuses on the crisis itself. Chapter 3 sketches the historical background and analyzes macroeconomic policies before and during the crisis as well as in the upswing; subsequent chapters cover the rapid growth after the recovery.

We begin by telling the story of the Finnish crisis in terms of shocks and policies and by providing an overview of the reasons behind the turbulent developments in Finland. We then offer a detailed diagnosis of the Finnish economic depression as a classic financial crisis. Brief comparisons will also be made with developments in other countries: in Chile, Mexico, some East Asian countries (Indonesia, Korea, Malaysia, and Thailand), and Sweden. Finally, and importantly, we do some econometric analysis of private consumption and investment behavior, to evaluate the role of interest rates and other financial variables in the Finnish real economy in order to explain the huge fluctuations in private investment and consumption behavior.

2.1   Boom, Bust, and Renewed Growth

Our overview of Finnish developments will be presented in two stages: overheating (1985–1990) and depression (1991–1993).[1] This section sets the stage for the more detailed analysis and discussion of the later sections and chapters.

Starting with the period preceding the crisis, we note that in the first half of the 1980s the performance of the Finnish economy, measured in terms of economic growth, was relatively smooth, with an average growth rate slightly above the OECD-European rate. Regarding the real GDP growth, figure 1.1 in chapter 1 gives the overall picture. The growth rate in Finland in the 1980s was higher than in Sweden and the EU-15 countries. This can be viewed as a catching-up process. Figure 1.1 also shows the relatively sluggish growth performance of the Swedish economy.

In contrast to most other European countries, Finland (and Sweden) did not experience any major rise in unemployment in the aftermath of the two oil crises of the 1970s. In the case of Finland, an important reason was the bilateral trade agreements with the former Soviet Union, which meant, for example, that an increase in oil prices automatically led to an increase in export demand. This isolated Finland from the oil price shocks and helped to stabilize the economy. The early 1980s can be characterized as a gradual disinflation period for Finland, and for other Western European countries, in the aftermath of the oil crises. There were no major indebtedness problems in the external dimension or in the public sector, and unemployment remained relatively low. Overall, the macroeconomic performance in this period can be viewed as broadly favorable.

2.1.1   The Overheating

The smooth ride began to get bumpy around 1986–1987. Economic growth accelerated significantly and the economy gradually entered a period of overheating. Several factors were behind this change. Without trying to quantify their relative significance, these can be categorized as follows:

1. Financial market deregulation, including both the abolition of regulation of domestic bank lending rates and, later, the lifting of restrictions on private borrowing from abroad, led to an explosion of domestic bank credit and large capital inflows, a significant fraction

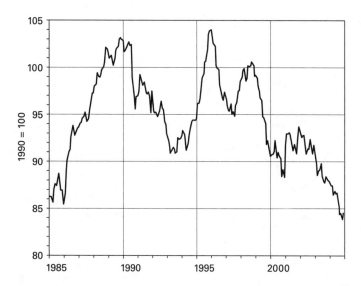

Figure 2.1
Terms of trade. *Note*: terms of trade represented by the ratio of export to import prices.
Source: National Accounts, Statistics Finland

denominated in foreign currencies and not hedged. We discuss these developments in section 2.2.

2. A sharp increase in the terms of trade resulted from a fall in energy prices and a rise in world market prices of forest products. The data on terms of trade is shown in figure 2.1.

3. Economic policies were not sufficiently restrictive to counteract the boom. These are discussed in detail in chapter 3.

The developments in the components of the GDP, together with their contributions to GDP growth, are shown in figures 2.2 through 2.4. The panel showing the contributions reveals that private consumption and investment had their biggest positive impacts during the boom. As figures 2.2 and 2.4 suggest, public consumption and public investment did not counteract the fast growth, but rather contributed to it. In the process of overheating, the rate of inflation rose from about 2 to 3 percent in 1986 to about 7 percent in 1989–1990; see figure 2.5. The figure also shows that the rate of unemployment declined from the about 4 percent in the first half of the decade to 2.5 to 3 percent at the end of 1989.[2] The Finnish boom led to high inflation and robust aggregate demand, which weakened the external balance and resulted in

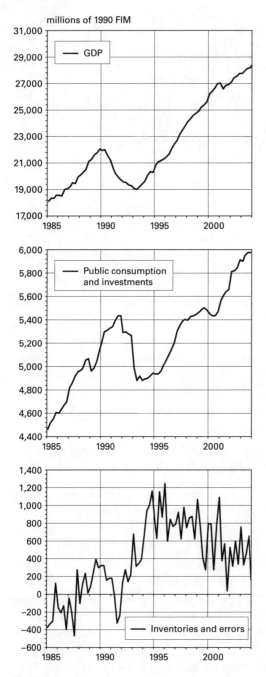

Figure 2.2
GDP, public consumption, investment, and inventories. *Source*: National Accounts, Statistics Finland

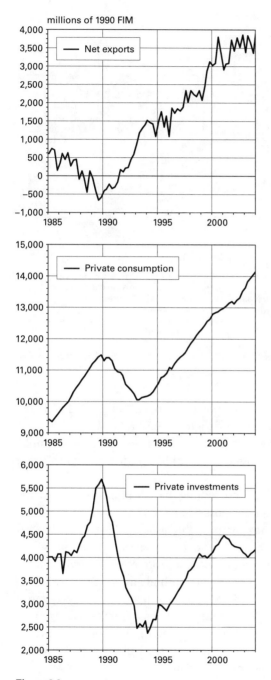

Figure 2.3
Next exports, private consumption, and investment. *Source*: National Accounts, Statistics Finland

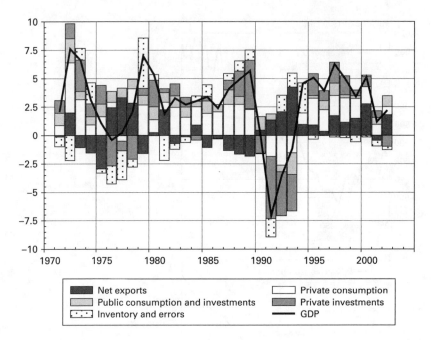

Figure 2.4
Contribution of demand components to GDP growth. *Source*: National Accounts, Statistics Finland

serious current account problems; see in figures 2.6 and 2.7. For 1985–1990, the average current account deficit-to-GDP ratio was 2.9 percent for Finland, while the corresponding figure for Sweden, for example, was only 1.1 percent, again suggesting that in Sweden the overheating was less pronounced.

During the boom, competition among banks intensified with the financial deregulation. The new possibilities for competition between banks led to increased risk-taking, probably as a result of moral hazard and myopic behavior.[3] As a result, indebtedness of the private sector increased significantly; see figure 2.13. Moreover, capital inflows increased hugely, partly as a result of the high interest-rate differential between domestic and foreign interest rates and partly because investors perceived a small likelihood of loss from exchange-rate movements. All this led to soaring real estate and other asset prices. The asset price developments will be discussed in section 2.3 in the context of our analysis of the financial crisis.

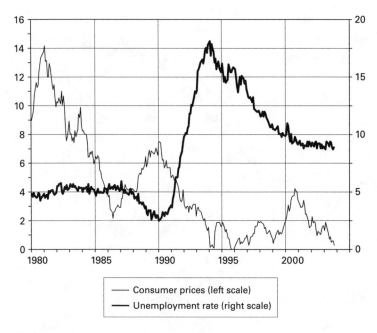

Figure 2.5
Inflation and unemployment. *Source*: Labor Force Survey and Consumer Price Index, Statistics Finland

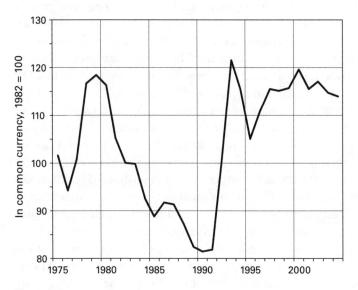

Figure 2.6
Relative unit labor costs. Competitor countries/Finland. *Source*: Statistics Finland and Eurostat

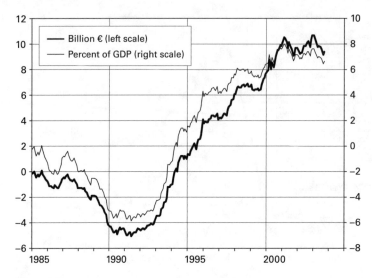

Figure 2.7
Current account. *Source*: National Accounts, Statistics Finland

2.1.2 Depression

The end of the boom came in 1990, and a rapid descent ensued. Economic activity, as measured by the growth rate of real GDP, declined swiftly from positive growth of 5.4 percent in 1989 to negative growth of −6.5 percent in 1991. As shown in figure 2.3, domestic private investment and private consumption fell sharply, while net exports of goods and services started to pick up. The decline continued, though at a slower pace through 1992 and most of 1993. The decline in GDP stopped and a turnaround took place in the fall of 1993.

While all domestic components of aggregate demand contributed to the decline in economic activity, it is evident from figure 2.3 that a particularly important feature was the huge decline in investment. Price inflation slowed down significantly and nearly vanished (see figure 2.5), which together with the depreciation of the Finnish markka after November 1991, led to a major improvement in the price competitiveness of the Finnish economy (see figure 2.6). As a result, the current account deficit gradually disappeared and shifted to surplus; see figure 2.7.

The emergence of a major banking crisis was a notable feature of the bust process. The rapidly falling asset prices and bankruptcies of firms led to credit losses, and the government had to provide public support for banks. These problems are discussed in detail in section 2.2. The banking crisis was an episode of significant financial restraint; like the overheating, it allows us to consider empirically the view that financial factors accentuated both the rise and the fall in the different components of aggregate private demand. In section 2.3 we elaborate on the effects of interest rates and other financial factors on both private investment and private consumption.

As we know, both international and domestic factors contributed to the onset of the crisis in 1991–1993. These factors can be classified as shocks and economic policy effects as follows:

1. Finnish exports to market economies declined as a result of slow international growth, loss in the price competitiveness of Finnish industry, and a decline in the terms of trade because the ratio of export to import prices decreased (see figure 2.1). With the collapse of the former Soviet Union, Finnish exports to and imports from Russia quickly dropped by 70 percent in 1991. This contributed to the decline in Finnish GDP in the crisis years, but—as we will argue—it is only part in the explanation for the depression.

2. After German unification, interest rates rose in Europe and, under free international capital mobility, also in Finland, as a result of more expansive fiscal policy combined with tighter monetary policy in Germany.

3. Monetary conditions became very restrictive in early 1989 due to an increase in real interest rates and appreciation of the Finnish markka.

Real interest rates rose dramatically from the start of 1990 until the end of 1992. This was due to defense of the Finnish markka against speculative attacks via higher nominal interest rates, and to the fall in the inflation rate at the onset of recession; see figure 2.8 for the interest rate differentials between Finland and Germany and figure 2.9 for real interest rates. The fixed exchange rate—that is, the hard-currency policy—ran into problems of credibility, and it was eventually abandoned with devaluation of the markka in November 1991 and floating of the currency in September 1992. Figure 2.10 shows the behavior of the exchange rate together with its bands up to 1992 (bands around the ECU central rate from 1996 are also shown). Fiscal policy was restrictive in 1991 and 1992, too, as will be discussed further on the basis of fiscal policy indicators in chapter 3.

While it is evident that both external shocks and domestic policies contributed to the onset of the Finnish depression, assessing their

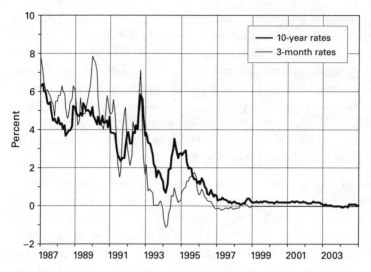

Figure 2.8
Interest rate differential, Finland vs. Germany. *Source*: Bloomberg

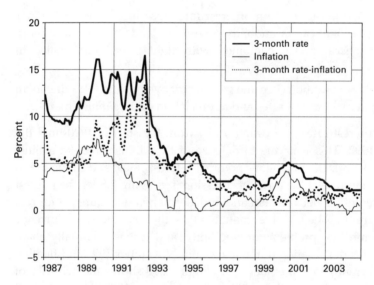

Figure 2.9
Real interest rate. *Source*: Bloomberg and Bank of Finland

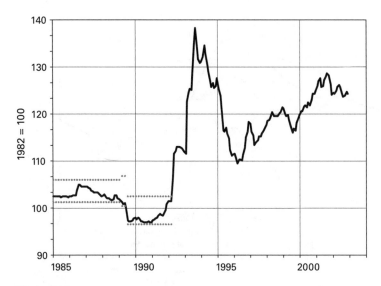

Figure 2.10
Bank of Finland currency index. Trade-weighted currency index. Rising curve indicates
FIM depreciation

relative significance is not straightforward. In our opinion, the external
shocks are not the whole story. A crude estimate of the effect of the
collapse of former Soviet Union trade could run as follows: in 1991
exports to the Soviet Union were around 15 percent of total exports,
and the share of total exports in the GDP was 23 percent. After allowing for a multiplier, it is likely that the 70 percent decline in this trade
can account for something like three percentage points of the total
decline of nearly seven percent in real GDP in 1991. Similarly, the
Western recession and the rise in interest rates in central Europe under
free capital mobility contributed to the depression, but they were also
only part the story.

In our view, financial factors indeed played a central role in amplify-
ing the effects of some shocks, especially those coming from the exchange rates and interest rates. Several financial market considerations
can be identified. First, the exchange- and interest-rate shocks, initially
due to defense of the hard currency (which led to higher interest rates,
as noted above) and subsequently because of a major depreciation of
the currency, must have influenced both consumption and investment behavior. These effects were significant, given the high levels of

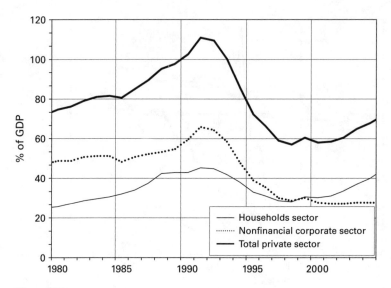

Figure 2.11
Sectoral debt ratios for Finland. *Source*: Bank of Finland and Statistics Finland

indebtedness of firms and households (see figure 2.11 for sector debt ratios in Finland) and given that a significant part of their borrowing was from abroad.

Second, the collapse of asset prices led to difficulties in the banking system and the emergence of a banking crisis. This crisis may have led to constraints on the financing of firms and households. We examine these issues in a more systematic way in the next section.

Third, the defense of the Finnish markka against speculative attacks boosted nominal interest rates, and when the inflation rate declined at the start of the recession, the real interest rate increased dramatically.

2.2   Financial Crisis

We have already suggested that financial factors were a key element in the Finnish crisis in the early 1990s, and we now examine this claim more closely. The roots of the financial crisis can be traced back to the deregulation of the financial system in the 1980s. That financial deregulation precedes a crisis has now been documented for many countries, including Chile in the early 1980s, Mexico in the mid-1990s, and most recently, several East Asian countries in the second half of the 1990s.[4]

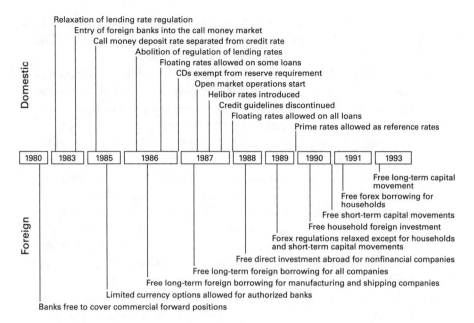

Figure 2.12
Deregulation of financial markets in Finland

We start by taking a detailed look at the financial developments. After that, we argue that Finland, like several other countries, faced problems of international indebtedness and liquidity at that time. Finally, we analyze the role of financial factors further by providing some econometric evidence of their importance for consumption and investment behavior.

2.2.1 Financial Developments

The process of financial deregulation began in the early 1980s, but the greater part of it was carried out in the second half of the decade. Liberalization of domestic financial markets and liberalization of international capital flows were implemented simultaneously when interest rates in Finland were much higher than abroad. This caused a massive capital inflow and led to uncontrolled credit expansion. (See figure 2.11, which describes the sectoral debt ratios in Finland. Figure 2.12, adapted from Vihriälä 1997, shows the timing of deregulation measures in 1980–1991, in both the domestic and international dimensions.) The deregulation process was problematic in several respects.

First, its timing in the second half of the 1980s coincided with the upswings of business cycles in Western market economies. The upswings increased incentives to borrow and thereby raised aggregate demand and the inflation rate. The coincidence of the international business cycle and financial market deregulation, as well as higher Finnish interest rates, gave rise to a big boom, soaring indebtedness in the private sector, higher relative unit labor costs, and a current account deficit. Later, it led to speculative attacks on the Finnish markka. Second, rules and practices in prudential regulation and bank supervision were left unchanged (see also Ahtiala 2006). These rules and practices were tightened only later in 1991, when the depression had already begun. Third, the tax system, which had favored debt financing of business and housing investment, was not reformed. Fourth, in the context of deregulation, lending rates were liberalized before deposit rates, which also helped to ease the banks' position. Finally, monetary policy (under a fixed exchange rate with a narrow band) tried to maintain some tightness in the wake of the boom, but this increased the interest-rate differential between Finland and Germany and provided further impetus to the large (in foreign-currency terms) inflow of foreign capital, which was already expanding as a result of a freeing of capital movements.

The capital inflows to the private sector were mediated largely by Finnish banks and also led to foreign-currency-denominated borrowing by firms, which were mainly operating in the nontradables sector. The Bank of Finland initially held the exchange rate in a narrow band, but as the demand for markkas increased in 1988, the band was first widened from ± 2.25 to ± 3 percent and then the markka was revalued by 4 percent in early 1989; see figure 2.10. Financial market deregulation contributed to exceptionally rapid growth in domestic bank lending; see figure 2.13. Much of the borrowing was for investments in real estate and other assets. For example, the share of deposit banks' credit to business and financial services in total corporate lending rose from 9.3 percent in 1985 to 22 percent in 1991. The rapid growth in lending in turn led to a doubling of real asset prices in the boom.

When the asset price bubble burst in the depression, banks were forced to reduce their lending activity, which aggravated the downturn. It took several years (to 1998) before banks' balance sheets had improved sufficiently to enable banks to significantly increase lending again; see figure 2.13.[5]

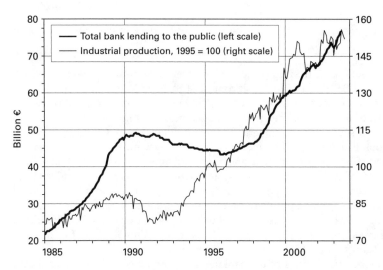

Figure 2.13
Bank lending and industrial production. *Source*: Bank of Finland and Statistics Finland

The banking crisis emerged as a part of the depression.[6] The onset of the banking crisis required major policy interventions by the government and Parliament. It also led to a major restructuring of the Finnish banking system. Box 2.1 describes the main policy actions and the restructurings.

A modest improvement in the banking sector took place in 1993, and further improvements came in 1994 and 1995. Loss making by banks did not end until 1996, and since 1997 the banks have showed significant positive profits; see figure 2.15. In the figure this development is illustrated by the negative net (accounting) profits, which were caused by the relatively higher credit and guarantee losses during 1991–1995. By contrast, the incomes and operating expenses of the banks showed only minor fluctuations.

The Finnish banking crisis was the result of several factors. The boom in the real economy in the 1980s, together with the speculative rise in asset prices and the rapid expansion of credit, rendered the banks vulnerable when the economy entered a downswing and asset prices started to fall. The very high real interest rates and the dramatic decline in asset prices contributed to liquidity and collateral problems and increased commercial bankruptcies, which in turn led to credit losses for banks, as shown in figure 2.15. The indebtedness problems

Box 2.1
Policy measures in the banking crisis and the restructuring of the banking sector in Finland

Policy actions to overcome the banking crisis began in September 1991 when the Bank of Finland took control of Skopbank, the "central bank" of the savings bank system. In early 1992 the government injected public funds, in the form of preferred capital certificates, into the banking system and set up a Government Guarantee Fund (GGF). GGF could use various instruments to support the banking system. As the crisis continued, first the government and then Parliament announced that the stability of the Finnish banking system would be guaranteed under all circumstances. In early 1993 the GGF was strengthened and it was given additional capital. Public support of the banking industry continued through 1994. The total fiscal cost of bank support is estimated at around 7.5 percent of the 1992 GDP.* (See Nyberg and Vihriälä 1994 for more details on support for the banking system.)

Major restructurings of the banking sector occurred during the crisis. First, most of the 250 savings banks were combined into the Savings Bank of Finland,** but subsequently this bank was split and the components merged with the commercial, and cooperative and the Post Office Bank. A small commercial bank, STS Bank, also merged with a big commercial bank (KOP), and KOP in turn merged with another big commercial bank (SYP) in 1995 to form Merita Bank. The structural changes continued with the recent merger of the remaining Finnish commercial bank (Merita Bank) with Nordbanken of Sweden in 1997. Another restructuring occurred in 1998 between the government-owned Post Office Bank and Vientiluotto (Export Credit Institution), which led to the creation of Leonia Bank.

In recent years, restructuring of the banking sector has continued as Merita-Nordbanken merged with a Danish and a Norwegian bank to form Nordea, a genuine Nordic Bank. Another merger occurred between Leonia Bank and Sampo Insurance Corporation, which created the Finnish "banking insurance conglomerate" Sampo. In autumn 2007 Danske Bank bought the banking operations of Sampo.

* For comparison we note that the corresponding figures for Sweden and Norway are 5.2 and 3 percent, respectively; see Edey and Hviding 1995.

** Only a handful of small savings banks have retained their independence.

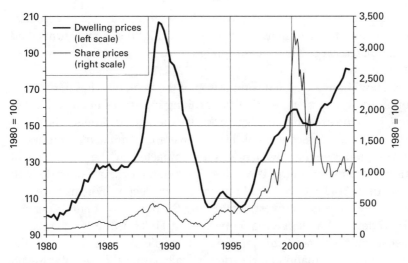

Figure 2.14
Real asset prices. *Source*: Bloomberg and Bank of Finland

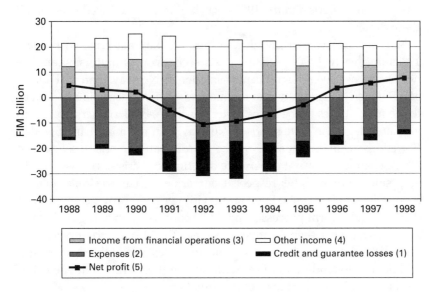

Figure 2.15
Indicators for banking crisis. *Source*: Statistics Finland

of the private business sector were also aggravated by the depreciation of the Finnish markka, because during the boom firms had
accumulated large amounts of foreign currency loans in the wake of
deregulation.[7]

Even without a detailed comparison of the banking crisis in different
countries, it may be noted that the banking industries in Nordic countries, with the exception of Denmark, all experienced similar crises. The
ratios of credit losses to bank lending were of similar magnitudes in
Finland and Sweden. Sweden was less impacted by the real effects of
crisis than Finland in the 1990s. For Finland, the collapse of trade with
the former Soviet Union made the recession deeper. For instance, the
cumulative decline in investment during the bust was about 25 percent
in Sweden and a staggering 50 percent in Finland (see Jonung, Schuknecht, and Tujula 2005). Jonung and Hagberg (2005) focus on the
experiences of Finland and Sweden by calculating the cost of crises in
the 1990s using three measures: loss of real income growth, loss of industrial production growth, and loss of employment growth. In Finland the cost of crisis in the 1990s was higher than in Sweden along all
these dimensions.

Norway also went through a systematic banking crisis in the late
1980s and early 1990s, and the crisis scenario was quite similar. The
net fiscal costs were significantly smaller in Norway than in Finland
and Sweden. This was due to the method of crisis resolution as well as
to the magnitudes of the crises. After the crises, bank ownership was to
a greater degree in state hands in Norway than in Finland and Sweden
(for comparison and analysis of the Nordic banking crises, see Sandal
2004). Denmark did not experience any financial crisis. This is remarkable, since in many other respects Denmark experienced similar macroeconomic developments. Edey and Hviding (1995) provide a review of
the financial reform processes in OECD countries. They argue that the
key difference between Denmark and the other Nordic countries lies in
the prudential supervision and disclosure rules and in the stricter capital adequacy standards in Denmark, where these were tightened con-
currently with financial market deregulation.[8]

2.2.2 International Indebtedness and Illiquidity

Analyses of financial crises in different countries have stressed that
problems of both international indebtedness and illiquidity are further
central characteristics of such crises and that these features largely result from an earlier real appreciation and lending boom after financial

deregulation; see, for example, Furman et al. 1998, Sachs, Tornell, and Velasco 1996, and Velasco and Chang 1998. We demonstrated earlier that Finland was experiencing real exchange appreciation and a borrowing boom both at home and from abroad, with a consequent worsening of international indebtedness. It is also of interest to consider whether Finland faced problems concerning international liquidity during the depression. In what follows, we briefly compare Finland's international indebtedness and illiquidity to those of Sweden, Mexico, Chile, and East Asian countries.

A country may be able to withstand a relatively high level of international indebtedness, provided its economic growth remains solid, the debt is largely long-term, and the confidence of international investors remains intact. Nevertheless, a high international debt position means increasing risks, should a country run into other economic difficulties. For Finland these risks were realized with the slowdown of the economy at the start of the 1990s. Table 2.1 shows the external debt-to-GDP ratio for Finland and Sweden for the period 1982–2001. For comparison, the table also shows the data for Chile (1984–2001), Mexico (1984–1993), Korea (1990–2001), and Thailand (1995–2001).

The buildup of international debt for Finland is much more pronounced than for Sweden because the Finnish current account deficits were much larger before the crisis.[9] This suggests that the external situation for Finland was relatively risky, so that the pressures mounted rapidly once the general outlook became gloomy in 1990–1991. International indebtedness for Mexico was very high in the 1980s and for Chile even higher in the mid-1980s. Thailand experienced a fairly rapid increase in its foreign indebtedness in 1997–1998. These indebtedness problems led to financial crises in these countries as well.

A country's international indebtedness includes both long- and short-run external liabilities. In contrast to debt, liquidity is exclusively a short-term issue and problems of international illiquidity can signal a financial crisis. A key issue is the mismatch of assets and liabilities. A country's financial system is internationally illiquid if its potential short-term obligations in foreign currency exceed the amount of foreign currency to which it has access at short notice. When governments are committed to act as lenders of last resort for the banking sector, deposits can be regarded as liabilities (see Velasco and Chang 1998 for more details). For this reason, the ratio of M2 money to foreign-exchange reserves seems consistent with the hypothesis of international illiquidity. This ratio is a commonly used indicator

Table 2.1
International indebtedness: Net foreign debt, % of GDP

	Finland	Sweden	Mexico	Chile	Korea	Thailand
1982	17	19				
1983	20	22				
1984	19	20	48	73		
1985	19	21	46	88		
1986	17	19	58	85		
1987	20	17	53	74		
1988	19	19	41	50		
1989	23	21	31	33		
1990	45	26	30	17	−32	..
1991	50	28	26	17	10	..
1992	53	23	22	14	11	..
1993	54	41	20	16	20	..
1994	63	45		..	23	..
1995	56	39		..	..	32
1996	54	39		..	..	35
1997	46	39		33,7	..	49
1998	87	38		37,7	..	57
1999	180	31		35,4	..	38
2000	140	25		37,1	..	48
2001	74	..		41,7	152	43

Sources: IMF.
Crisis: 1992–93 EMS crisis, 1994–95 Mexican meltdown and "Tequila Hangover," 1997–98 "Asian Flu." *Source*: FRB of San Francisco, Economic Letter, August 1998.
Countries affected by crisis. *Source*: *World Economic Outlook*, 1998.

for international illiquidity in the sense that the smaller the ratio, the higher the international illiquidity and vice versa. We now look at this indicator for Finland and compare it to some other countries that have experienced financial crises.

Table 2.2 shows that this indicator of international illiquidity for Finland not only exceeded one, but fluctuated in the second half of the 1980s with some increase in illiquidity at the onset of the crisis in 1990–1992. The behavior of the same indicator for Sweden is a bit different, but its behavior in the second half of the 1980s points to potential international illiquidity problems as well. Table 2.2 also provides indicator values for some other countries.

The conclusion we draw is that Finland experienced problems of international indebtedness and illiquidity during the crisis. These prob-

Table 2.2
International illiquidity

	Finland	Sweden	Mexico	Chile	Indonesia	Korea	Thailand	Malaysia
1980	11	21	19	2				
1981	14	19	19	3				
1982	14	17	65	5				
1983	16	13	11	4				
1984	8	14	7	3				
1985	7	9	9	3				
1986	18	10	6	3				
1987	7	10	3	4				
1988	9	10	3	4				
1989	11	9	6	4				
1990	7	6	6	3	5	6	4	3
1991	9	6	4	3	4	8	4	3
1992	12	5	5	3	3	7	4	2
1993	9	5	4	3	3	7	4	2
1994	5	4	19	3	5	6	4	2
1995	7	4	5	3	5	6	4	3
1996	9	6	5	4	5	6	4	3
1997	7	10	4	4	4	7	3	5
1998					3	4	4	3
1999					3	4	4	3
2000					3	3	4	3
2001					3	3	4	3

Sources: IMF.
Crisis: 1992–93 EMS crisis, 1994–95 Mexican meltdown and "Tequila Hangover," 1997–98 "Asian Flu." *Source*: FRB of San Francisco, Economic Letter, August 1998.
Countries affected by crisis. *Source*: World Economic Outlook, 1998.

lems contributed to the pressures on the Finnish markka and led to subsequent depreciations, banking-sector problems, and the breakdown of economic activity. The financial crisis in Finland had features similar to those not only in Sweden, but also in Chile, Mexico, Indonesia, Korea, Malaysia, and Thailand, though these features varied to some extent from country to country.

The impact of a crisis on subsequent macroeconomic performance is an important new concern, given the large number of financial crises in recent times. Among others, Ranciere, Tornell, and Westermann (2008) have presented a two-sector endogenous growth model in which financial crises can occur and have analyzed the relationship between financial fragility and growth. Their theoretical model shows why in countries with severe credit market imperfections, liberalization leads to higher growth and, as a by-product, to financial fragility. Using international data, they also show that there is a strong empirical link between growth and negative skewness of credit growth across countries (see table 1 in Ranciere, Tornell, and Westermann 2008, 11).[10] The case of Finland accords with such a view: as will be discussed later, Finland has become something of a "growth miracle" since the mid-1990s.

2.3   Econometric Evidence on Finance Constraints

It is often argued that financial crises involve significant financial restraint and possible illiquidity and that, in these periods, a banking crisis may lead to a credit crunch. This crunch, as well as high interest rates, may directly affect investment and consumption. In recent years there has been extensive research on the "credit-channel view," which argues that financial factors can indeed have a direct influence on business fluctuations in the real economy, as a result of capital market imperfections and agency costs in financial intermediation, especially in debt and bank lending.[11]

In this section we consider whether there is evidence of a credit crunch in the Finnish economy during the crisis in 1990–1992.[12] Such evidence of the credit channel would provide support for our thesis that a significant part of the Finnish depression was due to problems in the financial markets. Some econometric studies of the Finnish bank-loan markets have been carried out using 1990s data.[13]

Focusing attention only on bank credit may be a too-narrow approach. It is often argued that there exists a broad credit channel, implying that attention should be directed at the supply of funds in general.[14] This channel should manifest itself in the differential responses of external and internal finance as well as of small and large firms. The impact of financial factors on investment has been studied with microeconomic data for a number of countries, and Hubbard (1998) provides a review of the methodology and evidence. For studies that focus on consumption and financial factors, see, for example, Bacchetta and Gerlach 1997, Bayomi 1993, Wilcox 1989, and Zeldes 1989. In this section we look at Finnish evidence for the influence of financial variables on firms and investment as well as on consumption-savings behavior.

2.3.1 Cash Flow and Investment of Firms

We utilized a panel data set for the 500 largest Finnish firms to see whether evidence of the direct effects of financial factors on the investment behavior of firms can be found in Finland for the period 1986–2000.[15] Since the data cover only the 500 largest firms, it is not possible to consider the importance of size differences, which has afforded one way of testing the agency cost theory.[16] Nevertheless, it is possible to examine econometrically whether cash flow and other financial factors had an effect on the investment behavior of Finnish firms during the depression.

We estimated the standard model of investment and finance constraints from a panel constructed from the financial-reporting data set on Finnish firms. The same source has been used before by Ali-Yrkkö (1998) and Honkapohja and Koskela (1999). They had data up to year 1996 and found that cash flow had a stronger effect on investment in firms that they classified as financially constrained. Their conclusion was that financial constraints affected investment behavior and that a credit crunch amplified the effect of the macroshock that hit the economy in the early 1990s. Here, we update the calculations and use slightly different classifications of firms as financially constrained and unconstrained firms. Box 2.2 summarizes the setup.

We classify the financial constraints according to several alternative criteria. The first measure, similar to that of Bond and Meghir 1994, classifies a firm as unconstrained if it paid dividends but issued no new shares. The second criterion is similar but requires that the condition hold for both years t and t-1. The third criterion, following Whited 1992, classifies a firm as financially constrained if it has a high debt-to-assets ratio. We use an arbitrary cut point and split the sample into two equal-sized groups according to debt-to-assets ratios. The split is done using firm-years as observations, so that the same firm can be financially constrained in some years and unconstrained in others. The fourth criterion, also from Whited 1992, classifies firms according to the interest coverage ratio. Again we split the sample arbitrarily into two equal-sized subgroups. Finally, the fifth criterion attempts to measure credit ratings. We do not have a direct measure of credit rating by banks, so we use rankings given by a major business magazine, *Talouselämä*. Their measure is a weighted average of rate of return–to–own capital, solvency ratio (own capital / total capital), and gearing ratio (net debt / assets). Here we classify firms scoring below 5, on a scale

Box 2.2
An extended Euler equation for investment

The basic setup involves estimating Euler equations for investment following the specifications presented by Bond and Meghir (1994). From Euler equations one can derive an empirical investment equation

$$\left(\frac{I}{K}\right)_{i,t} = \beta_1 \left(\frac{I}{K}\right)_{i,t-1} + \beta_2 \left(\frac{I}{K}\right)_{i,t-1}^2 + \beta_3 \left(\frac{\pi}{K}\right)_{i,t-1} + \beta_4 \left(\frac{Y}{K}\right)_{i,t-1}$$

$$+ \beta_5 \left(\frac{B}{K}\right)_{i,t-1} + \beta_6 uc_{i,t-1} + d_i + \alpha_t + v_{it}$$

Here the investment–capital stock ratio (I/K) for each firm i in each year t depends on its lag and lag squared, its profits–capital stock ratios (π/K), sales/turnover–capital stock ratio (Y/K), and total debt–capital stock ratio (B/K). The other variables, $uc_{i,t-1}$, d_i and α_t, are the firm-specific user cost of capital, firm-specific factors, and time-specific factors. The term (π/K) controls for the role of cash flow, the output term (Y/K) for imperfect competition, and the debt term (B/K) for potential nonseparability between investment and borrowing decisions.

The Euler equation should hold for financially unconstrained firms, whereas for financially constrained firms the cash flow should have a positive effect on investment.

of 0 to 10, as constrained. Though not ideal, it can be argued that the measure does not deviate significantly from those used by banks for analyzing the creditworthiness of firms. Because all measures of financial constraints are only proxies for financial situation, one might expect that all firms are financially constrained to an extent, but the effect of the cash flow should be stronger for firms classified as financially constrained.

From the original data set, we eliminate those firms with missing values for key variables. Because our estimation method requires lagged values of the variables, we also exclude firms that do not appear in the data for the five consecutive years. To reduce the effect of influential outliers, we also exclude thirty-two firm-year observations with reported investments in excess of 35 percent of total assets. Table 2.3 shows the number of firms left in the data and the descriptive statistics on the variables that we use to classify the firms as financially constrained or unconstrained.

From table 2.3 one can immediately see that the sample firms were in much better financial shape at the end of the time period, which is

Table 2.3
Indicators of financial condition

Year	Number of firms	Paid dividends and did not issue new shares, %	Debt-to-assets ratio, annual average	Coverage ratio, annual average	Talouselämä ranking (scale 0–10)
1990	248	57.3	29.2	15.8	5.0
1991	290	51.3	30.8	38.7	4.7
1992	298	45.0	31.1	63.8	4.9
1993	295	38.6	30.0	37.0	5.2
1994	284	39.4	24.8	20.0	5.8
1995	283	51.2	22.6	12.9	6.5
1996	289	52.2	22.8	11.8	6.6
1997	280	55.7	19.7	5.5	6.9
1998	284	56.3	19.1	8.9	6.5
1999	234	62.8	17.6	7.3	6.8
2000	223	63.7	17.6	6.6	6.7

understandable. The worst years, in terms of financial situation, appear to be 1992–1994. For these years only slightly more than a third of the companies reported positive dividends and no new share issues. The corresponding figure is more than 60 percent for 1999–2000. The large Finnish companies were also highly indebted in the early 1990s. The average debt-to-assets ratio was around 30 percent, and it dropped below 20 percent in 2000. The improving financial health of the sample companies can also be seen from table 2.4, where we show the fraction of constrained firms according to the criteria presented earlier.

We estimated the investment equation, specified earlier in box 2.2, separately for the financially constrained and unconstrained companies. We first removed the company-specific error term by an orthogonal transformation (Bond and Meghir 1994) and included a full set of year dummies to capture the business-cycle effects. We then estimated the model by GMM using lagged values (t-2, t-3, and t-4) as instruments.

We first discuss results for the manufacturing firms. Focusing on manufacturing yields a more homogeneous sample where investment and financial data are more comparable. In table 2.5 (see appendix 2.1) we follow Bond and Meghir 1994 and classify the firms as unconstrained if they paid positive dividends and did not issue new shares.

Table 2.4
Proportion of constrained firms

	Fraction constrained according to different criteria, %				
Year	1	2	3	4	5
1990	42	58	58	49	44
1991	49	59	64	58	52
1992	55	63	62	54	46
1993	62	71	57	52	42
1994	60	71	46	39	32
1995	48	66	41	26	21
1996	48	59	40	22	21
1997	44	56	34	15	16
1998	43	55	32	18	20
1999	38	52	27	13	18
2000	36	45	24	16	21

Note: The numbers are not comparable to the previous table because of missing data on classification variables. Here any firm with a missing value in any classifying variable is excluded.

In columns 1 and 2, we use lagged values from periods t-2, t-3, and t-4 as instruments. In columns 3 and 4 the instrument set includes only lags t-3 and t-4, to avoid possible bias due to autocorrelation. The estimates for manufacturing firms generally have the expected signs but are not very precise. Cash flow has a positive effect on investment, and the effect is larger for the constrained firms, which accords with a natural hypothesis. Using only lags t-3 and t-4 as instruments yields much more imprecise estimates, though the ranking remains the same: cash flow has stronger effects for the constrained firms. Sales have a positive but insignificant effect for the unconstrained firms, while the effect is practically zero for the constrained firms. The coefficients of debt and user cost of capital are also insignificant.

Imprecise estimates are partly due to small sample size. Including all firms (not only manufacturing) increases the fraction of significant coefficients. We estimated similar equations for all firms using alternative criteria to classify the firms as constrained and unconstrained. Because we are primarily interested in the coefficients of cash flow, table 2.6 (appendix 2.1) reports only the estimated cash-flow coefficients for the different specifications. The cash-flow coefficients do not show a very systematic pattern but seem to be sensitive to the sample and the criteria used in classifying the firms. Our conclusion is that investments are more responsive to changes in cash flow in firms that are financially constrained, but the results are somewhat sensitive to the way firms are classified and to the samples used to estimate the model.

Our results are fairly similar to those in the other investment literature. For example, Kaplan and Zingales (1997) reanalyze the sample that Fazzari, Hubbard, and Petersen (1988) classified as financially constrained in their influential study. On the basis of the annual reports of these companies, they find that only for 15 percent of the firms is there any question of the firm's access to funds to increase investment, and more strikingly, that less financially constrained firms exhibit greater investment cash-flow sensitivity. Bond et al. (2003) studied the relationship between investments and cash-flow sensitivity using data from Belgium, France, Germany, and the United Kingdom, and showed that investments of UK firms are more sensitive to cash-flow fluctuations than in other countries. Mizen and Vermeulen (2005) used UK and German data to analyze the reasons for the cash-flow sensitivity of investment. They argue that creditworthiness is the main driver of cash-flow sensitivity.

2.3.2 Consumption, Net Wealth, and Financial Factors

The empirical overview, which we presented earlier, suggests that, besides private investment, private consumption also contributed to both the boom of the late 1980s and the downswing of the early 1990s. Therefore, it is also important to explore what happened regarding consumption behavior before, during, and after the crisis. We now look empirically at the determinants of the fluctuations in private consumption. We are interested in evaluating the effects of changes in net wealth and financial factors such as interest rates and credit constraints on consumption behavior. Box 2.3 summarizes the setup. Several relatively robust observations can be drawn from the estimations. The results are presented in appendix 2.2 and summarized in figure 2.16.

First, both wealth and disposable income have a positive effect on consumption, while the real interest rate turned out to be insignificant, confirming the view that it mainly affects consumption via asset values. Second, the effect of the nominal interest rate on consumption is significant and negative, reflecting liquidity constraints. Third, with a significantly positive effect, credit growth appears to be important as a determinant of consumption as disposable income. The short-run elasticities with respect to disposable income and credit growth are both in the neighborhood of 0.20.

Box 2.3
Net wealth, financial factors, and consumption

The starting point is the following consumption function, which can be regarded as an approximation to a much richer theoretical structure (see, e.g., Muellbauer and Murphy 1993 for further details, and Agell, Berg, and Edin 1995 for an application to Swedish data):

$$\Delta \ln C = \alpha_0 + \underset{(+)}{\beta}(\ln Y - \ln C_{-1}) + \underset{(+)}{(1 - \beta)\lambda}\Delta \ln Y$$

$$+ \underset{(+)}{(1 - \lambda)\beta\gamma W_{-1}/Y} + \underset{(?)}{(1 - \lambda)\beta\eta r} + other$$

Here C denotes private consumption, Y disposable income, W net wealth, and r the real interest rate. The equation has an error correction term, and β reflects the adjustment due to either habit formation or adjustment costs in consumption. A fraction λ of aggregate disposable income accrues to households that are subject to binding liquidity constraints, and the rest $(1 - \lambda)$ accrues to households that obey the permanent income hypothesis; see, for example, Campbell and Mankiw 1991. In the basic version for the first group of households, the rate of growth of consumption depends solely on the rate of growth in disposable income, while for the second group the real interest rate and the net wealth/income ratio play a potential role. As for the first group, private consumption may be affected by credit constraints via other channels as well. To the extent that lenders follow the practice of restricting borrowing so as to keep current payment–to–current income ratios below a ceiling level, the *nominal* interest rate affects the growth rate for aggregate consumption; see, for instance, Wilcox 1989. Moreover, other credit market variables such as credit growth and/or the wedge between borrowing and lending rate—which has been used in the literature as a measure of the tightness of credit conditions—may affect consumption growth. For international empirical evidence that aggregate consumption may be "excessively sensitive" to credit conditions as well as to income, see Bacchetta and Gerlach 1997 and Girardin, Sarno, and Taylor 2000.

To gauge the relative importance of various factors for fluctuations in private consumption we calculated the contributions of the explanatory variables. These are reported in figure 2.16.

The results in figure 2.16 can be summarized as follows. First, after the financial market deregulation in the late 1980s, credit growth contributed to private-consumption growth; the reverse occurred when the depression set in and in the late 1990s credit growth again contributed to consumption. Second, the role of the nominal interest rate

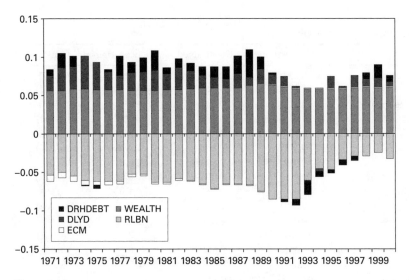

Figure 2.16
Contributions of explanatory variables for consumption growth. DRHDEBT = change in real aggregate household debt, DLYD = change in disposable income, ECM = error correction term (lagged consumption/disposable income), WEALTH = ratio of household assets to disposable income, RLBN = average rate of interest on new loans from depository institutions

increased in the early 1990s (a high interest rate reduced consumption), but the importance of interest rates declined after that. Finally, the relative effect of the wealth variable has been quite stable throughout the estimation period.

Appendix 2.1: Estimates of the Investment Function

The standard errors are large and the coefficients often insignificant. The point estimates indicate that cash flow has a positive effect on investment and that the effect is larger for constrained firms, which accords with a natural hypothesis.

We tried a number of other specifications—for example, differences instead of orthogonal deviations, simple fixed-effect estimators without lagged dependent variables, models without user cost, models that use only longer lags as instruments—and we estimated the models for various subsamples. We did not find any more stable patterns. In almost half of the different specifications the cash flow coefficient was larger for the unconstrained firms.

Table 2.5
Basic Euler equation results

	Unconstrained	Constrained	Unconstrained	Constrained
Investment	0.280	0.275	0.680	−1.037
	(0.151)	(0.127)*	(1.097)	(0.802)
Investment^2	−0.512	−0.463	0.453	3.613
	(0.445)	(0.270)	(3.585)	(2.261)
Cash flow	0.054	0.246	−0.327	0.399
	(0.114)	(0.104)*	(0.378)	(0.230)
Sales	0.017	−0.006	0.023	−0.005
	(0.011)	(0.015)	(0.020)	(0.027)
Debt	0.005	0.025	0.101	0.003
	(0.052)	(0.050)	(0.094)	(0.084)
User cost	−0.013	0.013	0.006	−0.366
	(0.084)	(0.137)	(0.225)	(0.541)
Constant	0.021	0.021	0.006	0.020
	(0.009)*	(0.011)	(0.016)	(0.022)
Observations	499	417	499	417
R^2	0.11	0.08		

Note: All explanatory variables are scaled by capital and lagged by one period. Year dummies are included in all equations.

Table 2.6
Effect of cash flow on investment

	All firms		Only manufacturing	
	Unconstrained	Constrained	Unconstrained	Constrained
Dividends > 0 and no new shares	0.159*	0.175*	0.054	0.246*
	(0.074)	(0.061)	(0.114)	(0.104)
Dividends > 0 and no new shares t and t-1	0.255*	0.163*	−0.034	0.235*
	(0.080)	(0.056)	(0.133)	(0.094)
Debt-to-assets ratio	0.204*	0.142	0.188	0.153
	(0.060)	(0.079)	(0.128)	(0.102)
Interest coverage ratio	0.174*	0.281*	0.176	0.271*
	(0.052)	(0.072)	(0.095)	(0.116)
Talouselämä rating	0.117	0.217*	0.228*	0.117
	(0.060)	(0.059)	(0.085)	(0.112)

Note: The equations include all variables in the previous table and the year dummies. The number of observations varies slightly because of missing data for some variables, but is on average about 3,000 firm-year observations when all sectors are included and about 1,000 for manufacturing.

Appendix 2.2: Estimates of the Consumption Function

All variables in the consumption-function specification, except the interest rate, are in logarithms. Variables also taking negative values have been rescaled prior to taking logarithms. We use annual data for the period 1971–2000. The dependent variable is the first difference of the log of private consumption, and we use two-stage least squares. The models were estimated using the method of instrumental variables. The instruments are lagged interest rates and lagged difference between banks' borrowing and lending rates. Following the suggestion

Table 2.7
Consumption function, dependent variable is the difference of private consumption LC

Variable	Coefficient	Std. error	t-value	t-prob
RLBN	−0.0062019	0.0013966	−4.441	0.0002
WEALTH	0.034703	0.023831	1.456	0.1578
D77	−0.047692	0.017515	−2.723	0.0116
LC_1	−0.0095073	0.0094562	−1.005	0.3243
DLYD	0.19294	0.032776	5.887	0.0000
DRHDEBT	0.19294	0.032776	5.887	0.0000

Additional instruments used: RLBN_1 RDIFF_1 (lagged variables of RLBN and RDIFF)
Specification $\chi^2(2) = 0.24875$ [0.6180]
Goodness of fit: $\chi^2(7) = 53.318$ [0.0000]
AR 1–2 F(2, 23) = 0.89257 [0.4233]
ARCH 1 F(1, 23) = 0.1205 [0.7317]
Normality $\chi^2(2) = 0.53454$ [0.7655]

Table 2.8
Consumption function, dependent variable is the difference of private consumption LC

Variable	Coefficient	Std. error	t-value	t-prob
RLBN	−0.0061261	0.0015585	−3.931	0.0006
WEALTH	0.011602	0.0030212	3.840	0.0007
ECM	0.0051079	0.0081206	0.629	0.5348
DLYD	0.19468	0.047038	4.139	0.0003
DRHDEBT	0.19468	0.047038	4.139	0.0003

Additional instruments used: RLBN_1 RDIFF_1
Specification $\chi^2(2) = 0.079161$ [0.7784]
Goodness of fit: $\chi^2(7) = 34.933$ [0.0000]
AR 1–2 F(2, 24) = 2.146 [0.1389]
ARCH 1 F(1, 24) = 0.60516 [0.4442]
Normality $\chi^2(2) = 1.3446$ [0.5105]

by Staiger and Stock (1997), the F-statistics for the first-stage regression (testing the hypothesis that the instruments do not enter the first-stage regression) were computed to examine the validity of instruments. The notation for variables is as follows:

LC   Private consumption
RLBN   Average rate of interest on new loans from depository institutions
DLYD   Change in disposable income
WEALTH   Ratio of household assets to disposable income
DRHDEBT   Change in real aggregate household debt
RDIFF   Difference between banks' borrowing and lending rates
ECM   Error correction term (lagged consumption/disposable income ratio)
D77   Dummy for year 1977

Diagnostic tests: AR 1-2 is the LM test for first- and second-order autocorrelation, ARCH 1 is the LM test for first-order conditional heteroscedasticity, the residuals are tested for normality using the Jarque-Bera test, and the specification test is an LM test for validity of instruments. The figures in square brackets are significance levels. The values of F-statistics for the first-stage regression (testing the hypothesis that the instruments do not enter the first-stage regression) were 69.57 and 62.287 for the two models, respectively, lending support to the validity of the instruments. We also checked the importance of the error correction term, but it was not statistically significant.

3   Macroeconomic Policies before and during the Crisis and in the Upswing

In this chapter we examine monetary, exchange-rate, and fiscal policies as well as wage policies carried out in Finland from the mid-1980s to the late 1990s in terms of their impact on macroeconomic performance. We will show that while the crisis in the early 1990s was caused by external factors, in particular the breakdown of the neighboring Russian economy and insufficient safeguards after financial market liberalization, it was aggravated by mistakes in macroeconomic policy. Both the fixed exchange-rate policy and pro-cyclical fiscal policies increased fluctuations during the overheating period in the late 1980s as well as during the crisis period in the early 1990s. In contrast, during the following upswing period macropolicies were largely appropriate.

3.1   Monetary and Exchange-Rate Policies

We begin with some historical background. Maintenance of a regime of fixed exchange rates was the cornerstone of monetary and exchange-rate policies in Finland for a long time in the postwar period. Through much of this period the Finnish economy was prone to periodic inflationary pressures, which in turn led to a deterioration of price competitiveness and to balance-of-payment problems. The external imbalances were corrected by major devaluations of the Finnish markka from time to time, for example in 1957, 1967, and 1977. Finland thus relied on a policy of fixed but adjustable exchange rates. The major devaluations, in the 30 percent range, often contained the seeds of a continued inflationary process and led to pressure for another devaluation in the future. However, due to the financial regulations—including the Bank of Finland's control of interest rates in bank lending and control of international capital movements—expectations of future devaluation did not affect domestic interest rates.

In the aftermath of the two oil crises of 1973–1974 and 1980–1981, a new regime for monetary and exchange-rate policy was established in an attempt to eliminate the inflation-devaluation cycle described above. This was executed by means of a new "hardened" fixed exchange-rate policy according to which the Finnish markka should be fully fixed, unlike in earlier periods. This policy was fairly successful for some years, though in the summer of 1986 there was significant speculation against the Finnish markka. This pressure was resisted and the exchange rate remained fixed for about six years. From October 1982 to November 1988 the markka was kept within a 4.5 percent band, after which the band was 6 percent from November 1988 to March 1989. See figure 2.10 in chapter 2 for the nominal exchange rate and its bands.

As we showed in the previous chapter, a major inflow of foreign capital to Finland occurred as a consequence of the liberalization of international capital flows in 1986–1987, when interest rates were much higher in Finland than abroad; see figure 2.8 in chapter 2. The fixed exchange regime gradually came under increasing pressure. The financial deregulation in the second half of the 1980s led to upward pressure on the Finnish markka. This pressure existed despite a current-account deficit as of 1987. Moreover, exports to the Soviet Union were gradually falling, which added to the overvaluation of the Finnish markka. In March 1989 the markka was revalued in response to the appreciation pressure, which exacerbated the international-competitiveness problem.

After the domestic boom ended, the markka became prone to speculative attack from 1990 onward. The monetary and exchange-rate policy response was to try to stick to the hard-currency regime, which led to very high domestic real interest rates. The fixed exchange-rate/hard-currency policy was eventually abandoned.[1] First, a forced devaluation of approximately 12 percent took place in November 1991 and then the Finnish markka was floated in September 1992. See Dornbush, Goldfajn, and Valdès 1995 for a critical discussion of this episode. They argue that "in this difficult setting the government made the surprising decision to peg the Finnish Markka to the European Currency Unit (ECU) without a priori devaluation.... The central bank and the government were quite wrong to overvalue the currency.... A shift to a more competitive currency, possibly accompanied by restrictive fiscal policy, would have helped to solve both the unemployment and the debt problems" (p. 235).

In the floating exchange-rate regime the Bank of Finland introduced a domestic inflation target. This rule gradually gained credibility. The interest-rate differential between Finland and Germany narrowed significantly (see figure 2.8 in chapter 2), indicating increased credibility and monetary stability. Some of the differential on long rates remained and actually widened temporarily in 1994, but this was brought under control by the fiscal policy package of the new government, which had taken office in spring 1995. Closer integration with Western Europe, with Finland joining the European Union in 1995, was also an important step in gaining credibility for the government. A major change in monetary and exchange-rate policy occurred in October 1996 when the floating ended and Finland joined the European Exchange Rate Mechanism (ERM). Subsequently (in 1998), Finland became a member of the Economic and Monetary Union, as the only Nordic country. This was the end of monetary independence for Finland.

It is evident that the fixed exchange-rate policy was clearly misguided on two occasions. First, with the exchange-rate fixed, domestic monetary policy could not counteract the boom during the financial deregulation period. Attempts to tighten monetary policy in 1988 led, under the fixed exchange rate, to a higher interest-rate differential between domestic and foreign rates, which further increased the inflow of foreign capital. Moreover, at the end of the boom the fixed exchange-rate policy had lost credibility and, as mentioned above, the Finnish markka was revalued in March 1989. This revaluation, forced by the large capital inflows, came far too late. An early revaluation of the currency in the boom and/or a move to floating (or active exchange-rate management) would have limited the capital inflows. We also note that as discussed in section 2.2.2, there is some evidence that Finland was moving to a position of international illiquidity; see table 2.2 in chapter 2.

The second failure of monetary and exchange-rate policy occurred in the wake of the depression. The fixed exchange rate was maintained in spite of all indicators pointing toward a serious downturn. The very high interest rates that came with the defense of the currency led to a tightening of monetary conditions, as can be seen in figure 3.1, which provides an index of monetary policy stance (calculated as the weighted sum of changes in a short-term interest rate and the exchange rate relative to values in a baseline year). These conditions contributed to a big collapse of aggregate demand in the highly indebted private sector. This development started in early 1990. The late

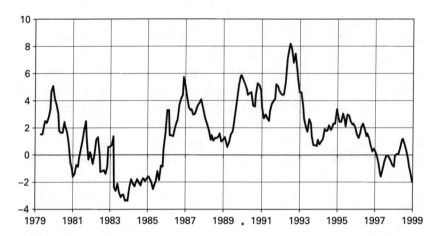

Figure 3.1
Monetary conditions index (MCI). Rising curve indicates tightening. *Source*: Mayes and Viren 2002

move to floating exchange rates initially worsened the situation, given the high, largely unhedged, foreign debts that had accumulated during the boom. However, floating subsequently permitted the easing of monetary policy and thereby contributed to the turnaround of the Finnish economy.

These two episodes provide a clear lesson. When financial deregulation is initiated there is a tendency for the external value of the home currency to appreciate due to capital inflows. Under such circumstances, the currency should be floated so that its appreciation can mitigate the overheating due to financial deregulation and curb capital inflows. In our view, the Finnish boom-bust cycle would have been less extreme under a floating exchange-rate regime, though the precise extent of mitigation is debatable. However, we would emphasize that financial deregulation, along with failures in macroeconomic policy, led to the lending boom in both domestic and foreign-currency terms when interest rates in Finland were much higher than abroad.

The floating exchange-rate regime, together with inflation targeting in monetary policy, were important elements in the recovery of the economy from the deep depression. These policies gradually strengthened credibility and thus contributed to macroeconomic stability in Finland. They were one part of the economic policy package aimed at getting the fundamentals right. In part, this policy enabled Finland to

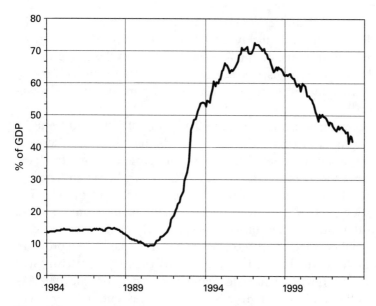

Figure 3.2
Central government debt/GDP ratio. *Source*: Statistics Finland

join the European Union in 1995 and the Economic and Monetary Union when it was launched in 1999.

3.2 Fiscal Policy

The crisis in the early 1990s had a major impact on the government budget. As background, it should be recalled that the size of the public sector in Finland, as measured by total public expenditure relative to GDP, has traditionally been below the OECD-Europe average. During the crisis, the GDP share of the public sector increased dramatically, starting in 1990. Figure 2.2 in chapter 2 makes it clear that public consumption and public investment declined in real terms in 1991–1993. However, total expenditure (even without banking support) increased mainly as a result of increased transfers, especially unemployment compensation.

This increase in total expenditure, together with a fall in tax revenues, led to a sharp increase in the budget deficit, to 10–15 percent in 1992–1993. In turn, an explosion of central government debt emerged, which was also affected by bank support; see figure 3.2 for developments in central government debt. With falling real GDP, the debt-GDP ratio shot up quickly, and as a result Finland shifted from the group of European low public-debt countries to the group of medium debt countries in just a few years. This development also meant that throughout the crisis the rising central government debt was a major concern.

A new government was formed in the spring of 1995, and from the start it adapted a program of fiscal consolidation covering its term in office. Clearly, an important impetus to this program came from the requirements for membership in the EMU, which began to loom on the political horizon after Finland became a member of the EU. The consolidation program was well received in the financial markets and therefore the interest rate differential versus Germany dropped dramatically in the spring of 1995; see figure 2.8 in chapter 2. The program led gradually to smaller deficits and, with resumption of real GDP growth, central government indebtedness started to decline 1997. As fiscal consolidation and fast growth continued, the central government deficits gradually diminished and turned into budget surpluses in 1999; see figure 3.3.

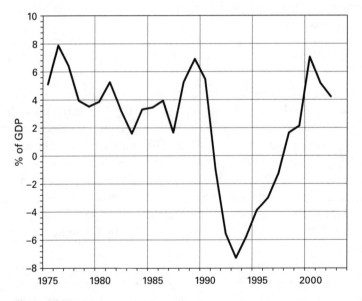

Figure 3.3
Central government net lending

To assess the stance of discretionary fiscal policy, the fiscal impulse is defined as the discretionary change in the budgetary position of the government, excluding the effects of business cycles on the government budget. There are several specific definitions in the literature:

1. The simplest possible definition of the fiscal impulse is the change from the previous year in the primary budget deficit as a share of GDP.

2. Blanchard (1993) suggested estimating what government expenditures and revenues would be in a given year if the unemployment rate had remained the same as in the previous year. This means that the measure of fiscal impulse is constructed as the difference between this unemployment-adjusted measure of the primary deficit and the previous year's primary deficit.

3. The third measure, often called the OECD measure (see, e.g., Alesina and Perotti 1995), defines the fiscal impulse as the difference between the current primary deficit and the primary deficit that would have prevailed if expenditure in the previous year had grown with potential GDP, and revenues had grown with actual GDP. Thus this measure also takes the previous year as the benchmark year.

4. The IMF measure differs from these in that it assumes as the benchmark year not the previous year but a reference year in which potential output is close to actual output.

We feel that a disadvantage of the IMF measure is the arbitrariness of the choice of the benchmark year. Therefore, we present the fiscal impulse measures 1–3 in figure 3.4. Interpretation of the change in fiscal stance is as follows: fiscal policy is loose (tight) if the difference from one year to the next is positive (negative).

These fiscal impulse measures behave qualitatively similarly during the period of interest. Therefore, in what follows we use the measure suggested by Blanchard (1993) to gauge discretionary fiscal policy. Figure 3.5 describes the Blanchard fiscal impulse measure as a share of GDP together with a change in unemployment rate. Looking first at the period of overheating before the crisis, it is seen that, according to the Blanchard measure for discretionary fiscal policy, fiscal policy was expansionary in 1987 but turned slightly restrictive in 1988–1989. During the latter period the contribution of public consumption and public investment to economic growth also declined.

During the crisis, discretionary fiscal policy was at first expansionary and thus countercyclical in 1991, and in 1992 it tightened a bit despite

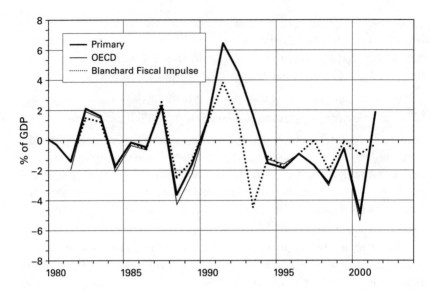

Figure 3.4
Three indicators of fiscal policy. *Source*: Bank of Finland

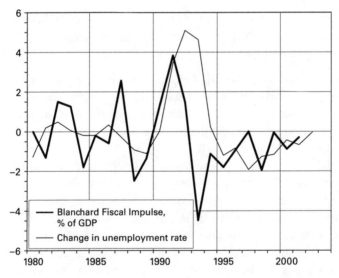

Figure 3.5
Indicator of fiscal policy and change in unemployment. *Source*: Bank of Finland

the increase in unemployment. Unemployment continued to increase in 1993–1994, but discretionary fiscal policy remained tight, particularly in 1993. During this latter period, government support of banks and the effects of automatic stabilizers were counteracted by cuts in government expenditures and increases in tax rates. The restrictive effect of government expenditures can also be seen from the contribution of public consumption and public investment to GDP growth, which was highly negative in 1993, as shown in figure 2.2 in chapter 2. According to the Keynesian view, this means that during the Finnish economic crisis fiscal policy was not consistently designed for stabilizing aggregate demand.

One can argue that at "moderate" levels of public debt, expansionary fiscal policy raises aggregate demand, according to the Keynesian view. But when high deficits increase the level of government debt, fiscal policy might have anti-Keynesian effects by affecting private-sector expectations of future income from labor and capital. At "very high" levels of government debt, the private sector might expect that, with a high probability, they may have to pay extra taxes in the near future, so that aggregate demand declines. Using OECD data from nineteen countries including Finland for the period 1965–1994, Perotti (1999) presents strong evidence that expenditure shocks have Keynesian effects at low levels of central government debt, and anti-Keynesian effects in the opposite circumstances.[2] Therefore, with a high level of public debt, it is important to start fiscal consolidation and not continue with fiscal expansion.

As a general conclusion regarding countercyclical fiscal policy, it is evident that fiscal policy was generally not systematically countercyclical; see figure 3.5. In the 1980s boom, discretionary fiscal policy was only weakly countercyclical, and during the depression period its bias seems to have fluctuated in a somewhat inconsistent manner. The big deficits and the jump in public-sector indebtedness during the crisis were quite remarkable. In such a crisis policymakers face the difficult problem of identifying the permanence of shocks to the economy. In the case of Finland the shock from the collapse of trade with former Soviet Union seemed at least semipermanent, but the other shocks also appeared to be essentially cyclical.

The clear plan of fiscal consolidation and its systematic execution were evidently an important part of macroeconomic policies aimed at good fundamentals to secure robust economic growth. It is noteworthy that government budgetary balance and improved public-sector indebtedness took several years to achieve. This is due in part to the fact that structural unemployment increased during the crisis (see Honkapohja and Koskela 1999, section 5, as well as chapter 7 of this book).

Next, we present what are, in our opinion, the lessons from the Finnish experience for macroeconomic management, for example for several new EU countries.

3.3   Lessons for Macroeconomic Management from the Finnish Experience

We begin with the crisis years of the early 1990s. Our analysis and interpretation of the reasons behind the Finnish depression can be aptly summarized as "bad luck and bad policies," as first suggested in Honkapohja and Koskela 1999. The external shocks were exogenous to the Finnish economy and in this sense unavoidable. The collapse of trade with the former Soviet Union in 1991 was the biggest negative shock, but as noted in chapter 2, two other important international developments can also be identified. First, in the second half of the 1980s the Western economies experienced a strong business-cycle upswing, which for Finland meant a considerable increase in the terms of trade. Second, the recession in the Western market economies in the early 1990s and the high interest rates due to the monetary-fiscal policy mix associated with German unification were additional negative external shocks. As we have seen, Sweden in the early 1990s provides another good example of the classic financial crisis. Sweden suffered less in economic terms that did Finland in the 1990s because of no dependence on trade with the former Soviet Union. For Finland, the cost of the crisis in the 1990s was higher than for Sweden in terms of real income growth, industrial production growth, and employment growth (see Jonung and Hagberg 2005).

Clearly, the external shocks played a significant role in the Finnish boom-to-bust process—the "bad luck" part of the economic deterioration. However, external shocks are not nearly the whole story. If there had been no additional factors, Finland would have experienced a recession, but not a severe depression.

We have argued above that Finland experienced a classic financial crisis. These problems originated from a poorly designed deregulation of the financial system and a lack of other reforms that would have been needed in conjunction with the financial deregulation. Lifting domestic interest-rate controls, allowing the private sector to borrow freely from abroad, and sticking to the fixed exchange rate gave rise to a lending boom at home and from abroad, much of which was in foreign currencies.[3] In the case of Finland, this lending boom was made worse by an ill-advised tax system that favored debt finance and outmoded bank regulations. For all these reasons, the private sector became financially highly vulnerable to changes in interest rates as well as in the exchange rate.

A situation of financial vulnerability means that when the turnaround occurs and/or the currency becomes subject to speculative attack, only bad options are available to the policymakers. Defense of the Finnish markka led to a tightening of monetary policy, and the consequent rise in domestic interest rates hurt the domestically highly indebted private sector. Moreover, the currency devaluation—aimed at bolstering the weakened competitiveness of the export sector—was effectively a capital levy on that part of the private sector that had borrowed in foreign-currency terms. Both of these policy choices were grim for a country spiraling into economic crisis, and Finland in the early 1990s was no exception.

The failure to reform the regulatory regime of the financial markets and the decision to leave the tax system unchanged in the process of financial deregulation were clearly policy errors for Finland. We would emphasize that financial market deregulation should not be carried out in isolation; it must be tackled in conjunction with reform of the tax system and tightened bank supervision. These measures can mitigate the domestic and foreign lending booms, which stem from deregulation.

Next, we evaluate macroeconomic policies, which in Finland contributed to fluctuations in the financial system and thereby affected both cyclical and structural unemployment—that is, consumption, investment, and wage and price setting.

Looking at monetary and exchange-rate policy, we have seen that the strong Finnish markka policy was misguided at least twice: at the start of the boom and again in March 1989 when the end of the upswing was in sight. The failures of exchange-rate and monetary policy present a clear lesson. When financial deregulation is initiated, there is a tendency for the external value of the home currency to appreciate due to huge capital inflows and to the fact that usually—as for instance in Finland—fiscal policy does not offset the demand-augmenting effect of the capital inflow. To mitigate overheating from financial deregulation and liberalization of capital movements, one should let the currency float (and most likely appreciate at least initially). Then when the turnaround begins, the financial system will be less fragile and the authorities will have more favorable options for dealing with the evolving problems.

An early floating of the home currency appears to be an appropriate complement to financial deregulation. If the currency is not floated during the deregulation phase, then the options for a mix of exchange-rate and monetary policy will all be bad. Monetary policy becomes ineffective, and attempts to rein in the boom lead to larger capital inflows, which then render the financial system even more fragile if investors wishfully think the likelihood of exchange-rate movements is very small. Currency depreciation via floating would seem a necessity after a boom when competitiveness has deteriorated. After the float, the credibility of monetary policy can be improved by setting a clear domestic target, such as an inflation target. If it is not overly tight, monetary policy should contribute to recovery, because inflation will normally not be a problem in a depression.

For fiscal policy the broad lessons from the Finnish experience are in principle straightforward. First, fiscal policy restrictiveness should complement any financial liberalization phase to mitigate the boom. Second, if a crisis and depression nevertheless emerge, big deficits and a jump in public-sector indebtedness are perhaps inevitable. This makes it imperative to pursue fiscal consolidation at some stage of a major crisis. Such a change in fiscal policy increases credibility, thereby lowering domestic interest rates and paving the way for recovery. Of course, the timing of the consolidation is a knotty problem. It hinges on the nature of the impulse shocks. If the shocks are essentially cyclical in nature, a policy of fiscal smoothing would seem natural. Then the economy will have to live with fairly sizable public deficits and some buildup of public debt. However, if the shocks are deemed permanent or semipermanent, the fiscal adjustment should not be delayed too long.

Improved monetary credibility via inflation targeting and a systematic program of fiscal consolidation clearly played a role in the turnaround and resumption of economic growth in Finland in the mid-1990s. Membership in the EU and then in the EMU also contributed to economic growth, being signs of macroeconomic stability and growth-oriented economics. The second half of the 1990s can be largely seen as a period of implementing the clear general policy goals.

Coupled with luck, structural developments and growth-oriented structural policies set off a virtuous cycle and the Finnish miracle came into being. The following chapters examine the structural changes in detail and assess the economic policies pursued in Finland over the period from crisis to rapid growth.

Before ending this chapter, we briefly characterize what happened in terms of wage negotiations.

3.4   Wage Policy

In Finland, binding wage bargains are negotiated at the industry level between the unions and employer organizations. These agreements specify a general wage increase that applies to all wages within a sector. A typical agreement also defines a set of minimum tariff wages that apply to each job. Collective agreements cover the union members (currently some 75 percent of all employees) and nonunion members in the sectors where union density exceeds 50 percent. Due to this extension of the union contracts to nonunion workers, the union contracts cover roughly 95 percent of all employees. In contrast to many other countries, the Finnish wage-bargaining system is still very centralized (see OECD 2004, 141). Most bargaining rounds start with negotiations between confederations of employer and employee unions, creating a high degree of coordination in the individual union contracts. Union bargains have then been negotiated on the basis of the wage increases, specified in the central agreement.

According to theoretical results and empirical evidence based on cross-country comparisons, centralized bargaining tends to moderate wage increases (see, e.g., Calmfors 2001 and Flanagan 1999). The time-series evidence from Finland supports this evidence (Uusitalo 2004). Even though the Finnish wage-bargaining system has been classified as being among the most centralized in cross-country comparisons, there has been considerable variation in the degree of centralization between the different bargaining rounds. During the past thirty years, there have been seven bargaining rounds (1973, 1980, 1983, 1988, 1994, 1995, and 2000) in which no central bargain was reached and bargaining occurred at the industry level. These industry-level bargains have led to significantly higher wage increases than the centralized bargaining rounds have. The result also holds after controlling for macroeconomic conditions prevailing during the wage negotiations. Moreover, if the centralized bargaining rounds are classified according

Table 3.1
Nominal wage increases by level of wage bargaining

Raw averages	Number of cases	Bargained wage increase	Nominal wage growth
Decentralized bargaining	7	6.5	10.1
Centralized bargaining (all)	27	4.7	8.9
Degree of centralization			
No coverage (decentralized)	7	6.5	10.1
Low coverage	3	8.4	13.3
Medium coverage	10	6.6	12.0
Wide coverage	14	2.5	5.1
Controlling for unemployment and inflation	Number of cases	Bargained wage increase	Nominal wage growth
Decentralized bargaining	7	7.7	12.2
Centralized bargaining (all)	27	4.4	8.1
Degree of centralization			
No coverage (decentralized)	7	7.3	11.8
Low coverage	3	7.1	10.6
Medium coverage	10	5.5	9.5
Wide coverage	14	3.2	6.7

Source: Uusitalo 2004.

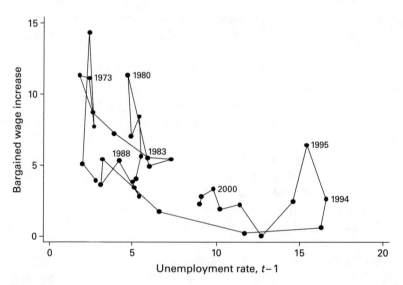

Figure 3.6
Wage growth and unemployment. *Source*: Uusitalo 2004

to coverage, the average wage increases have clearly been for the bargaining rounds with the widest coverage. Table 3.1 shows these results.

Figure 3.6 illustrates the relationship between degree of centralization and wage growth by plotting the bargained wage increases against the unemployment rate prevailing at the time of wage negotiations. The figure shows a clear Phillips-curve relationship between the wage increases and unemployment. Comparing the wage increases in the industry-level bargains of 1973, 1980, 1983, 1988, 1994, 1995, and 2000 to the centralized bargains reveals that wage growth tends to be higher with industry-level bargaining than in the other years with similar unemployment rates.

The results with Finnish data are consistent with those from cross-country data, according to which centralized bargaining moderates wage growth and thereby reduces the equilibrium unemployment rate. Prime examples from the 1990s include national bargains in the recession years 1992 and 1993, when nominal wages did not increase at all. On the other hand, different rates of economic recovery across industries led to industry-level bargaining and somewhat higher wage increases in 1994 and 1995.

Labor market programs and reforms are another aspect of policies to combat unemployment. Concerning active labor market programs, the share of labor market training increased in the 1990s when the depression began. The total number of individuals in such training was highest in 1997, at more than 4 percent of the labor force. Naturally, participation in training programs slightly improved labor market prospects, but overall the labor market institutions did not change much in the 1990s (see, e.g., Koskela and Uusitalo 2006).

4 Renewed Growth and Structural Change

In earlier chapters we discussed how Finland went through the most severe recession of its economic history in the early 1990s. Fortunately, the recovery that began in 1994 was also rapid. The average growth rate of the Finnish economy during the period 1994–2001 was 3.3 percent per year, which was the second highest among the fifteen Western EU countries, after Ireland. Employment grew by approximately 2 percent per year during the same period. Growth has slowed since the burst of the ICT bubble in 2001, and employment has remained almost constant. In 2005, employment began to increase again.

Part of the recovery was due to the forces of a normal business cycle. The recession left the economy with a large amount of idle resources and, once the growth picked up, some of these resources were put back to productive use. In what follows, we estimate the size of the output gap and calculate the fraction of growth that can be explained by the return to a more normal stage of the business cycle. However, there is more than the business cycle to the recovery story. This is because the 1990s were also a period of rapid restructuring of the economy. Resources were reallocated among the sectors and firms within the sectors, which helped increase productivity growth. This creative destruction process had already begun in the mid-1980s, but reallocation of resources among firms has boosted productivity over the entire period from the 1980s to the present.

In this chapter we proceed as follows. We start by providing output-gap estimates for Finland in order to distinguish between cyclical and structural components of recent economic growth. We then compare the Finnish growth performance to other industrial countries. Next, we examine productivity growth in the 1990s and discuss the important role of the mobile phone sector. We also demonstrate that there has been a change from extensive growth due to an increase in the capital-labor ratio to intensive growth due to a change in total factor productivity. Then we describe changes in the structure of employment during the recession and recovery and evaluate the effects on the growth rate. Finally, we briefly characterize the internalization of Finnish corporations in terms of FDI and employment.

4.1   Aggregate Developments

4.1.1   Increased Capacity Utilization After the Recession: Output Gap Estimates for Finland

If recovery from recession was an important part of the favorable economic performance during the second half of the 1990s, then a large fraction of the growth in output can be attributed to business-cycle fluctuations. It is not easy to break the changes in output down into cyclical and trend components empirically. Still, for example, the OECD routinely carries out this process by calculating the "output gap," which is the difference between output and potential output at a stage where resources are fully utilized. Currently, the OECD uses an approach where structural unemployment is an unobserved variable that is related to the change in inflation according the Philips curve (OECD 2004). Our estimates are based on a similar idea with some modifications. Box 4.1 describes the methods that we apply in more detail.

The output-gap estimation results can be characterized as follows. First, the estimate of the linear trend in output (2) indicates that Finnish real GDP has grown annually on average by 2.4 percent during the period 1975–2002. The coefficients of the autoregressive part suggest that deviations of output from potential output tend to be fairly persistent. Moreover, as mentioned in box 4.1, the coefficient of the bank-lending variable is positive and thus indicates that deviations of the growth rate of bank lending from its long-run average tend to magnify the output gap. If bank lending grows faster than average in the previous quarter, then actual output tends to exceed the potential level in the current period, which happened during the boom period in the late 1980s, while the reverse was true during the recession of the early 1990s. Finally, the coefficient of the output-gap variable in the inflation equation indicates that inflation accelerates if the lagged output gap is positive, and vice versa if the lagged output gap is negative.

The estimates of the potential output and the output gap are presented in figures 4.1 and 4.2. For comparison, we also add in figure 4.1

Box 4.1
Measuring potential output and output gaps

There are several alternative approaches for estimating potential output. The most often used method is the Hodrick-Prescott (HP) filter (Hodrick and Prescott 1997). Essentially, this is a time-series technique that creates smoothed series. The degree of smoothness, set by the researcher, determines how closely the filtered series follow actual developments. However, such filtering techniques are not well suited for periods that may contain structural breaks. If the smoothing parameter is given a high value, the filter reproduces the actual series; if the smoothing parameter is given a low value, the filtered series exhibits trendlike behavior. Neither adequately captures structural breaks.

Our estimation procedure is based on unobservable-component techniques. We use an extended version of a bivariate model of Kuttner 1994. The basic idea in that paper is that inflation depends on the difference between actual and potential output. By specifying a time-series process for potential output, it is possible to estimate the output gap based on changes in the inflation rate.

We start with the identity

(1) $y_t \equiv x_t + z_t$

where y_t is seasonally adjusted log real GDP, defined as the sum of the potential output x_t and the output gap z_t. Next, we assume that potential output follows a random walk with drift

(2) $x_t = x_{t-1} + \mu_x + \varepsilon_t$

where μ_x captures the rate of growth of potential output. We postulate the following time-series process for the output gap:

(3) $z_t = \phi_1 z_{t-1} + \phi_2 z_{t-2} + \lambda q_{t-1} + u_t$

Equation (3) slightly modifies the original Kuttner approach. According to (3), the output gap follows a stationary AR(2) process with two stochastic inputs, (i) an exogenous variable q_{t-1} and (ii) the white-noise term u_t. The variable q_{t-1} describes the lagged demeaned growth rate of bank lending to the private sector and proxies the effect of financial shocks on output. According to this hypothesis, financial-sector behavior affects the business cycles (see, e.g., Kiyotaki and Moore 1997 and Carlström and Fuerst 1997). This variable turns out to be statistically significant and improves the estimation of the output gap, suggesting that financial market shocks, particularly in the banking sector after financial deregulation, were an important determinant of the output gap.

Finally, we specify an aggregate supply relationship or Phillips curve that relates inflation to the lagged output gap as

(4) $\pi_t = \mu_{\pi,t} + \beta z_{t-1} + v_t$

(5) $\mu_{\pi,t} = \mu_{\pi,t-1} + \zeta_t$

Box 4.1
(continued)

In equation (4) π_t is the rate of inflation, as measured by $100 \times \log(CPI_t/CPI_{t-1})$, where CPI_t is the consumer price index. Because there are some apparent gradual long-run shifts in the Finnish inflation rate that cannot be associated with the output gap, the intercept term in (4) is specified as a local-level parameter in equation (5).*

The model specified above can be represented as a state-space model, which can then be estimated by the maximum likelihood method through an application of the Kalman filter.

* Historical inflation rates in many OECD countries display long-run patterns that cannot be attributed to the output gap, and so they should be removed from the inflation rate when estimating potential output and output gap. Previous studies have done this implicitly using various techniques. Kuttner (1994) applied the growth rate of inflation (which is one way to remove smooth long-run patterns from the inflation rate), while Gerlach and Smets (1999) used a detrended inflation rate. The local-level modeling approach applied here has an advantage over previous approaches in that it enables estimation of the trend path of the inflation rate simultaneously with the output gap.

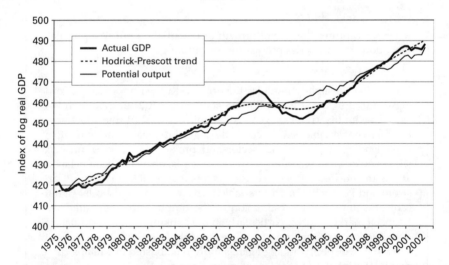

Figure 4.1
Actual output and potential output estimates

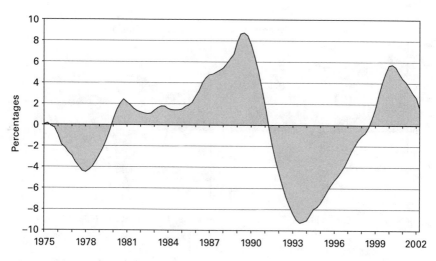

Figure 4.2
Output gap

a conventional HP-filter estimate of potential output. As shown in the figure, the HP-filter estimate closely follows the actual output, with a major deviation occurring only during the overheating period in the late 1980s and during the severe recession in the early 1990s. According to the HP-filter estimate, potential output decreased slightly from 1990 to 1994 and then increased rapidly. We think that our unobserved-component technique of characterizing potential output over the period of the financial crisis is more realistic than HP estimates.

The potential output series produced by the unobserved-component technique behaves in a very different way from what we have just seen. According to the estimates, potential output has grown over the whole period, with a brief pause at the start of the 1990s. The growth rate of the potential output series was roughly the same in 1980s and 1990s. A crucial difference is also that according to the HP-filtered estimate, actual and potential output were equal in 1996, implying that the output gap had closed, while the estimate based on the unobserved-component technique indicates that the output gap was closed only in 1999. The first years of the new millennium were boom years, and actual output was again above potential output.

Figure 4.2 reveals that actual output exceeded potential output for most of the 1980s. The sharp turnaround in the cycle is illustrated by the swing in the output gap. Actual output dropped from 8 percent above to 8 percent below potential output level between the boom

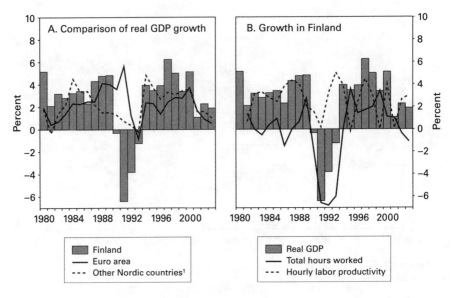

Figure 4.3
Comparison of real GDP growth. Weighted average for Denmark, Iceland, Norway, and Sweden using 1995 GDP and PPPs. *Source*: *OECD Economic Surveys*, Finland, December 2004

year 1989 and the trough of the recession in 1993–1994. The figure also reveals that if we wish to examine economic changes in the 1990s that were not affected by the stages of the business cycle, a comparison between 1991 and 1999 or 2002 would be appropriate choices, because actual output was then close to potential output.

4.2   Finnish Growth Performance from an International Perspective

As one can see from figure 4.3, Finland's long-term growth profile has been very volatile in comparison with the euro area and other Nordic countries. The recession in the early 1990s was much larger than in the other euro-area countries and the recovery was more rapid. After the mid-1990s, Finland's GDP growth per capita was higher than in most other OECD countries. Even though the employment rate also increased by about 2 percent per year, the main source of Finland's GDP per capita growth during this period was the increase in labor productivity (measured by GDP per hours worked). Between 1994 and 2003 the increase in labor productivity contributed, on average, 2.5 percent to annual GDP growth rate. As one can see from figure 4.4,

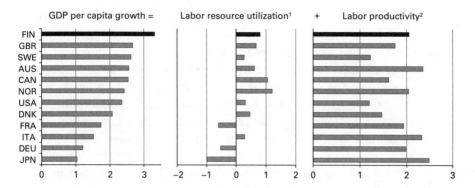

Figure 4.4
Sources of growth. Percent per annum average, 1994–2003.
1. Labor resource utilization measured as total number of hours
2. Labor productivity measured as GDP per hour worked.
Source: OECD Economic Surveys, Finland, December 2004

both the growth in labor productivity and GDP per capita were among the highest in the OECD. The increase in labor input had a significant effect up to the year 2000. After that, employment growth halted and the total hours worked decreased in 2002 and 2003.

Given the rapid growth of the Finnish economy after the economic crisis in the early 1990s, Finland's average living standard (as measured by GDP per capita in purchasing-power parities) is now higher than the EU average. Finnish GDP per capita is higher than in the United Kingdom and Germany and only slightly lower than in Norway, if the oil sector is excluded, but still significantly lower than in the United States.

When assessing aggregate labor productivity levels and growth rates one should, however, consider that there tends to be an inverse relationship between labor productivity per hour and labor resource utilization. Dismissing less skilled workers increases labor productivity, while integrating those workers into the labor market reduces productivity. In the first case GDP per capita will decline despite higher aggregate productivity (as labor resource utilization declines), while in the second case GDP per capita increases as a result of higher labor resource utilization. Looking at figure 4.4, it appears that many European countries, including Finland, have indeed increased their aggregate level of labor productivity per hour by reducing employment of less skilled workers, and some other countries have gone even further than Finland in this respect. For example, in France, Germany, and

Norway labor resource utilization is lower than in Finland, while the levels of labor productivity per hour are higher. Part of the higher aggregate productivity levels in these countries may therefore be explained by lower resource utilization. Differences in labor resource utilization are, however, not the only reason productivity levels and growth differ across countries and over time. Labor productivity can be enhanced by increasing the capital stock (capital deepening), by modernizing it by innovation, or by improving the skill level of the labor force (human capital). We show later that an important part of Finland's good growth performance during the past decade can be explained by these latter factors, in particular innovation and improved human capital.

4.3   Productivity Growth in the 1990s

The most important reason for Finland's growth performance after the mid-1990s was the rapid growth of labor productivity. Since 1976, labor productivity has grown in the whole economy at an average annual rate of 3.1 percent. Excluding nonmarket activities, where productivity growth cannot be adequately measured, labor productivity growth over the last twenty-five years has been, on average, 4 percent. In the 1990s productivity growth was highly volatile. It was highest during the crisis in the early 1990s when employment was sharply reduced. During the 1990s as a whole, average labor productivity growth was approximately equal to that of the previous decades, as shown in figure 4.5.

Even though the growth of labor productivity was, on average, not higher in the 1990s, the nature of the productivity growth has changed remarkably. Later, we present the following findings: (1) productivity growth was heavily concentrated in some industries, (2) productivity growth changed from extensive growth due to increasing capital intensity to more intensive technical progress, (3) productivity growth benefited from reallocation of resources toward more productive firms, and (4) improvements in the quality of labor increased productivity growth.

4.4   High Growth in the Mobile Phone Sector

During the 1990s economic growth was concentrated in a very narrow sector, namely, manufacturing of electrical and optical equipment. The

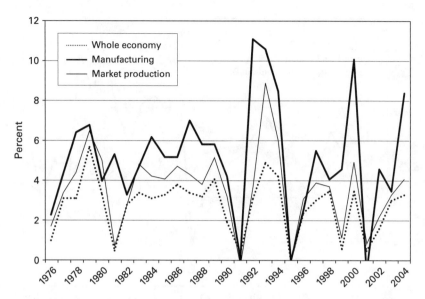

Figure 4.5
Annual growth of labor productivity. *Source*: National Accounts, Statistics Finland, ASTIKA database

annual growth of output in this sector exceeded 20 percent between 1993 and 2000. A significant fraction of this growth was due to just one company, Nokia, which became very successful in the mobile phone industry. In chapter 6 we analyze the reasons behind the success of the Finnish New Economy and Nokia and their contributions to growth.

The high growth in the electrical and optical equipment industry was the driving force of growth in the total manufacturing sector, while growth in the rest of the manufacturing sector was very low. Even before the 1990s, growth in the electrical and optical equipment industry was higher than in the rest of the manufacturing sector. However, its share was low and its contribution to the growth of total manufacturing was small; see figure 4.6 for details.

With much higher growth rates than the rest of the manufacturing sector, the electrical and optical equipment industry has also contributed to the labor productivity growth of total manufacturing in recent years. For example, in 1998 and 1999, almost all of the productivity growth of the manufacturing sector was due to productivity growth in the electrical and optical equipment industry.

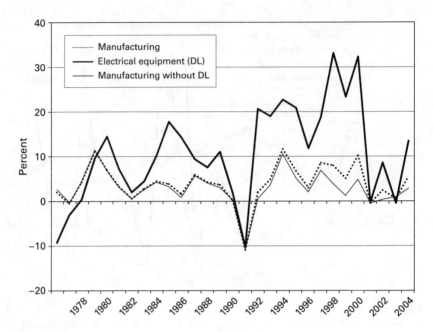

Figure 4.6
Annual growth of output in manufacturing. *Source*: National Accounts, Statistics Finland

4.5　From Extensive to Intensive Growth

Perhaps the most important development in productivity growth has been a shift from extensive growth due to an increase in the capital-labor ratio to intensive growth due to a change in total factor productivity (TFP). For the period from 1976 to 1990, the increase in the capital-labor ratio accounted for two-thirds of the labor productivity growth. Since 1994, changes in the capital-labor ratio have not contributed to labor productivity growth, which has been totally due to more efficient use of inputs and technical progress.

The early 1990s were very volatile in terms of productivity growth. Capital intensity increased in 1992 and 1993 as a result of falling employment, not because of an expanding capital stock. Between 1993 and 1999 capital intensity increased in market production, on average, by only 0.2 percent, and after 1994 it declined as the capital stock increased less than the labor input. By contrast, TFP growth accelerated in the 1990s. The average growth rate of TFP between 1975 and 1990 was 1.8 percent in market production, but between 1993 and 1999 growth rate of TFP was, on average, 4.4 percent. These numbers sug-

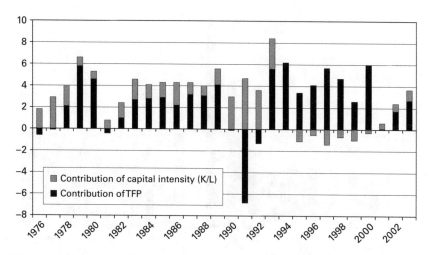

Figure 4.7
Labor productivity growth in market production. Contribution of capital intensity is obtained by deducting TFP growth from labor productivity growth. *Source*: Tuottavuus-katsaus 2004, Statistics Finland, National Accounts 2004

gest that the nature of growth in the 1990s has been remarkably different from past decades. The contribution of capital was much lower and the contribution of TFP much higher; see figure 4.7.

Compared to other OECD countries, TFP growth has been very high in Finland, and particularly impressive in the 1990s. As one can see from figure 4.8, only in Ireland did the TFP growth rate exceed the Finnish rate. This result is consistent with a recent study by Annenkov and Madachi (2005), who compared labor productivity growth in Finland and the other Nordic countries to the large euro-area countries, using data extending to the year 2004. In their comparison, too, the Finnish productivity growth rate between 1996 and 2004 is the highest among the countries compared. And they also find that high productivity growth in Finland is mainly due to TFP growth. In their growth assessment, the TFP contribution to labor productivity growth in Finland is higher than that of any other country included in the comparison.

4.6   Creative Destruction in Action

Aggregate productivity may increase via two different mechanisms. Productivity in existing plants increases when the firms reorganize

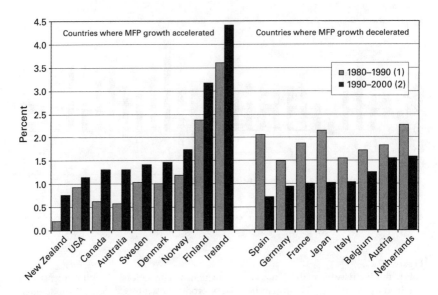

Figure 4.8
Multifactor productivity growth accelerated in some countries. Business sector, based on cyclically adjusted series, 1980s and 1990s.
1. 1983–1990 for Belgium, Denmark, and Ireland, 1985–1990 for Austria and New Zealand
2. 1990–1996 for Ireland and Sweden; 1990–1997 for Austria, Belgium, and New Zealand; 1990–1998 for Netherlands, 1990–1999 for Australia, Denmark, France, Italy, Japan; and 1991–2000 for Germany
3. Western Germany before 1991.
Source: OECD (2000)

production in a more effective way and when they adopt more effective technologies. Aggregate productivity also increases when resources are reallocated from less productive to more productive sectors or plants. Reallocation occurs as the existing plants expand or contract, and new plants start up and old plants shut down. This reallocation of resources increases aggregate productivity if the expanding or entering firms have higher levels of productivity than the contracting or exiting firms.

A recession may increase the future growth path by accelerating the reallocation process toward more productive firms as the less productive firms exit the market. The short-term effect of a recession is to both increase job destruction and reduce job creation, so that total job reallocation may not change immediately. However, once the recovery picks up there are idle resources that can be employed by the more productive plants.

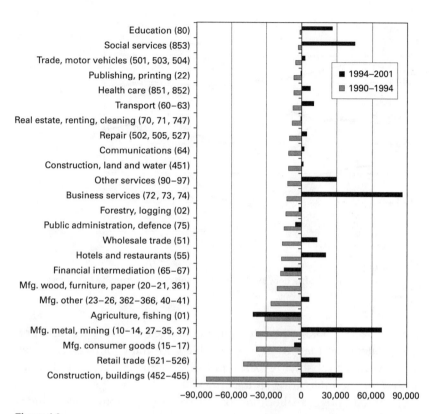

Figure 4.9
Change in employment by industry during recession and recovery. *Source*: Own calculations based on data from Labor Force Survey. Industry classification according to ISIC 2–3 digit classification as used in LFS

Figure 4.9 examines big structural changes in employment in Finland by sectors during the downturn of the early 1990s and the following recovery period. As figure 4.9 indicates, the newly created jobs were rather different from the jobs of the early 1990s. The first thing to note is the concentration of job losses in some industries. During the four years of economic crisis, 450,000 jobs were destroyed. Total employment declined by 18 percent from the 1990 level. Half of the jobs in construction disappeared between 1990 and 1994. Employment also declined by approximately 25 percent in manufacturing, retail trade, hotels and restaurants, and financial services.

Once employment started to increase after 1994, the largest increases occurred in services. Employment in manufacturing also grew rapidly, but this was largely due to the growth in the electronics industry (the

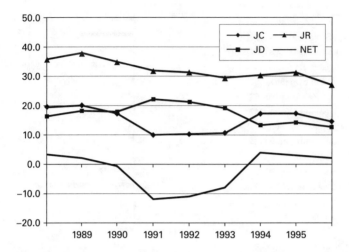

Figure 4.10
Job creation and job destruction, 1988–1996. JC = job creation rate, JD = job destruction rate, JR = job reallocation (JC+JD), NET = employment change (JC−JD)

Nokia effect). Looking at employment changes within more disaggregated categories than what was possible with the Labor Force Survey data would probably reveal rapid restructuring across industries within the manufacturing sector.

As noted above, reallocation of the resources among sectors hides large changes occurring within these sectors. It is possible to define sectors at a more disaggregated level and examine the changes in employment across two- or three-digit industries, or even across individual firms or individual plants within firms. Such calculations have been performed for Finland by a number of authors. Figure 4.10 reproduces the figure by Ilmakunnas and Maliranta (2000). They calculate job destruction (JD) and job creation (JC) rates in the whole private sector over the period 1988–1996. As seen from the figure, the job destruction rates increased during the recession years 1991–1993. At the same time, the job creation rates decreased. Both the increase in job destruction rate and the decrease in job creation rate contributed to the net employment change (NET). In fact, the contributions of the changes in job destruction and creation were roughly equal. Interestingly, the total job reallocation (JR) rate—defined as the sum of the job creation rate and the job destruction rate—did not increase during the recession, but rather displays a declining trend over the whole period. The impact of reallocation on productivity growth can be examined by break-

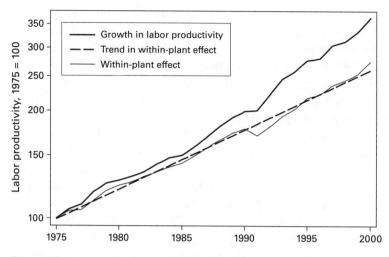

Figure 4.11
Growth in labor productivity, 1975–2000. *Source*: Maliranta 2004

ing productivity growth down into within-plant productivity growth (within effect) and the effect of reallocating resources across plants (between effect).

To identify more fundamental changes in productivity, some aggregation over time is required. Therefore, many studies present productivity calculations as averages over several years or smooth time series by using moving windows. Another and perhaps more illuminating way of aggregating over time is used in a study by Maliranta (2003). He calculates the cumulative effect of aggregate productivity growth and the part due to productivity growth within firms (within effect). Figure 4.11 reproduces the results of these calculations for labor productivity in manufacturing between 1975 and 2000. The calculations define an index that equals 100 in the base year 1975 and update this index by the annual productivity growth rates.

An analysis of the results for labor productivity reveals that within-plant productivity has very closely followed a log-linear trend over the whole period. Within-plant productivity growth has been on average 3.8 percent per year. However, starting from the mid-1980s aggregate productivity growth has been substantially faster than within-plant productivity growth. The widening gap between the two series indicates that the acceleration of labor productivity growth since the mid-1980s can be largely attributed to the reallocation of resources among plants. Böckerman and Maliranta (2007) break the productivity growth components down further by using data disaggregated to the regional level. The overall picture is not fundamentally changed, but the authors find that the between effect displaying the effects of resource reallocation between plants was particularly strong in Southern Finland.

The corresponding calculations can also be done for the cumulative effect of growth in TFP (see Maliranta 2003). The calculations show that TFP grew only slightly between 1975 and 1991. As noted in the previous section, most of the growth in labor productivity during this period was due to an increase in capital intensity. However, after 1991, the TFP growth rate increased rapidly. In fact, the capital-labor ratio decreased for most of this period, so that most of the growth in labor productivity was due to an increase in TFP. In addition, the gap between within-plant and aggregate productivity growth is higher in TFP than in the aggregate productivity. Thus, reallocation of resources among plants had a large impact on TFP—that is, on technical progress during the 1990s.

In this chapter we have reviewed some evidence for the effects of creative destruction on productivity growth. We have noted that reallocating resources among firms by simultaneous job destruction and job creation accelerates productivity growth if the growing firms are more productive than the contracting firms. This effect seems to have been reasonably strong in Finland in the 1990s. In fact, an international comparison by the OECD using firm-level data shows that Finland is the only country in the study where resource reallocation among firms has had a consistently positive effect on labor productivity (see OECD 2001a).

The Finnish recession provides an interesting case study for the impact of reallocation on productivity growth. However, it turns out that contrary to what one might expect, the recession itself was not a particularly intense period of restructuring. Job destruction rates increased, but because job creation simultaneously decreased, conventional measures of reallocation do not indicate particularly rapid reallocation between firms. However, after the recession, productivity growth—especially growth of TFP—increased rapidly. This was largely due to an increase in the effect of reallocation. A conclusion drawn by Maliranta (2003) was that reallocation had become more selective, so that firm growth became more closely correlated with productivity level. Possible explanations for why this might have occurred are that higher competition in product markets and increased requirements for asset

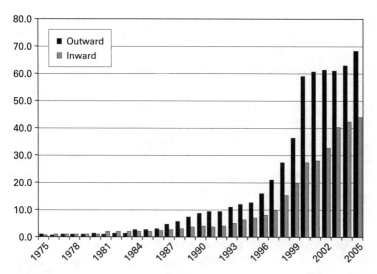

Figure 4.12
Stocks of outward and inward FDI for Finland 1975–2002. Billion € in 2002 prices

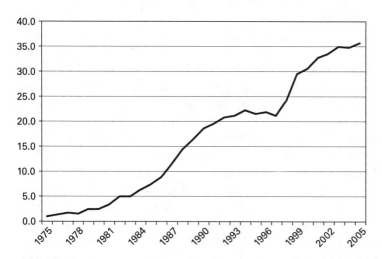

Figure 4.13
Share of foreign affiliates' employment in total employment of Finnish manufacturing enterprises (%). *Source*: Bank of Finland and ETLA

returns in financial markets fostered reallocation of resources toward the most productive firms.[1]

4.7 Internationalization of Finnish Corporations

As in some other successful countries like Sweden, internationalization of Finnish corporations has also been one of the fundamental changes occurring in the Finnish economy. This trend strongly increased in the 1990s, as reflected in the sharp increase in foreign direct investment as well as in the employment of foreigners by Finnish firms. In this section we present a brief overview of the internationalization of the Finnish economy (see Mannio, Vaara, and Ylä-Anttila 2003 for further details).

In the 1970s, Finnish firms' international activities consisted mainly of exports, with few sales offices or production units abroad. Capital controls were lifted and foreign ownership was liberalized in the early 1990s. The gradual financial market liberalization, which began in the mid-1980s, also increased firms' direct access to foreign capital markets and positively affected internationalization. The foreign direct investment statistics (see figure 4.12) illustrate the increasingly rapid internationalization of the Finnish economy, in particular from the mid-1990s on. Between 1996 and 2002, outward FDI flows relative to GDP, led by the metal and engineering industries, increased on average by around 10 percentage points, whereas before that the ratio had been very low. The starting point for internationalization was to expand in traditional export markets like Sweden, Germany, and the United Kingdom.

In the 1990s many of the large Finnish firms were transformed into multinational enterprises with substantial foreign ownership, headquartered abroad, and with a substantial part of their production capacity outside of Finland. This was reflected in a sharp increase in foreign employment, as figure 4.13 shows. This development was even more pronounced for large Finland-based firms. While the share of foreign personnel of the ten largest firms was less than 15 percent in 1983, it increased to over 60 percent in the year 2002.

5 The Importance of Human Capital

In chapter 4 we noted that the growth of labor productivity in Finland has been higher than the OECD average for the period 1994–2003. One of the key factors in the growth of labor productivity is an increase in the skill level of the labor force. In this chapter we describe recent changes in the educational level of the labor force and evaluate the effects of the improvement in education on productivity growth. In the next chapter we examine the effects of investments in research and development.

Investments in education can be considered investments in human capital. Accumulation of human capital increases productivity and contributes to economic growth. Even if such investments are subject to diminishing returns, a more highly skilled labor force will achieve higher levels of income in the long term, and during the transitional period the growth rate will also be higher. According to endogenous growth theory, the growth rate could even be permanently higher if the higher skill level leads to more intensive research or facilitates the adoption of new technologies, both of which cause technological progress to accelerate (for a theoretical analysis of this issue, see, e.g., Barro and Sala-i-Martin 2004, chapter 5).

There is thus strong theoretical support for a key role for human capital in the growth process. However, measuring its impact on overall productivity growth is not easy. In addition to the direct effects, which can to some extent be measured, there may be indirect spillover effects. In competitive labor markets workers are paid according to their marginal productivity, so that the productivity effects of human capital can be measured by wage differences. However, if there are spillover or external effects, an investment in human capital by some workers also boosts the productivity of others (for a theoretical analysis of the social returns of human capital investment, see, e.g., Acemoglu 1996). In this case the person making the human capital investment does not receive all of its benefits—the social return to human capital investment is then higher than the individual return. Unfortunately, these social returns are hard to measure. Since no one receives all the benefits from investment in human capital, there are no natural measures of the impact of human capital investment.

The Finnish performance in investment in education has been impressive. As we will demonstrate in this chapter, the rate of increase in the general education level has been among the fastest in the OECD countries. The higher level of education has contributed to an increase in the skill level of the labor force. The youngest cohorts of workers in Finland are now among the most educated in the OECD countries. The youngest cohorts are also among the top performers in international skill comparisons such as those of the International Adult Literacy Survey. The trend toward increasing skill levels appears to be continuing. In recent PISA studies, Finnish fifteen-year-olds scored highest among all participating countries in both reading and mathematics. This is remarkable given that the Finnish expenditure on education, measured by share of GDP or spending per pupil, is only around the OECD average.

In this chapter we proceed as follows. First, we look at the skill level of the Finnish labor force and how it has changed during the past decade, and we make comparisons with other OECD countries. Second, we discuss the impact of education on productivity and the merits of the Finnish educational system.

5.1   Skill Level of the Labor Force

During the 1990s the quality of labor input changed rapidly in Finland. In 1990, more than a third of workers had no education beyond the compulsory level. By 2003 the proportion of the least educated workers had fallen below 20 percent. The decrease in the share of workers with the lowest educational level was accompanied by increases in the percentage of workers with secondary and higher education. Figure 5.1 displays these trends by reporting employment shares by educational level. A rough calculation that allocates to each educational level a standard length of schooling shows that between 1990 and 2003 the average length of education increased by 0.85 years. This is probably an underestimate, since the length of compulsory education has also

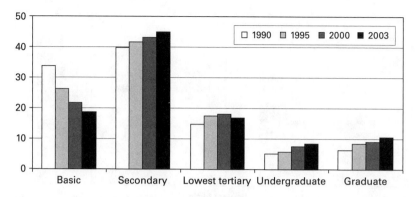

Figure 5.1
Employed by level of education. *Source*: Own calculations based on microdata from Income Distribution Survey

increased over time. If more educated workers are more productive, an
increase in the average educational level leads to a larger increase in effective labor input than a simple calculation of working hours would
indicate.

It is rather surprising that the educational level of the labor force
can change so rapidly in a relatively short period of time. In fact,
the change is a product of two factors. First, the expansion of the educational system has increased the educational level of younger generations. When younger generations gradually replace older ones, average
education increases. The fraction of Finnish students that continue
their education to the higher levels has increased rapidly since the
1970s.

Second, changes in relative employment rates have also played an
important role. Unemployment rates rose much more rapidly for the
least educated workers during the recession in the early 1990s. Also,
the least educated ones more often moved out of the labor force, in
particular, in the older age groups. The employment rate of those with
only basic education fell from 52 to 37 percent between 1990 and 1995.
The decline in the employment rates for the more educated workers
was much smaller even during the recession of the early 1990s. Figure
5.2 reports changes in these employment rates by level of education.

Hence, part of the increase in the average educational level of
employed workers, and therefore, part of the increase in labor productivity can be explained by the exit of less skilled workers from the labor
force. Even though lower employment rates among the less educated

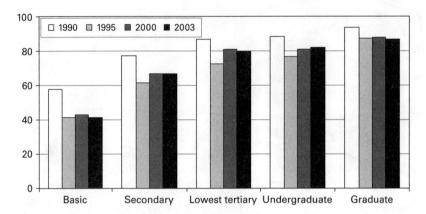

Figure 5.2
Employment rates by level of education. *Source*: Own calculations based on microdata from Income Distribution Survey. Employment rates are calculated for working age population (15–64).

may increase average labor productivity, the effect on GDP per capita is clearly negative, because less of the labor potential is employed.

5.2   Comparison with Other OECD Countries

According to OECD estimates, the level of education in Finland, measured by average number of years of education for the working-age population, has increased by roughly two and a half years over the past three decades. The level of education of Finnish adults is now at a level similar to that in Denmark but still lower than in Sweden, Norway, and some other OECD countries, including Germany, the United Kingdom, Canada, and the United States (table 5.1).

OECD comparisons of average educational level are problematic because educational systems in different countries are very different. Simple indexes, such as average years of education, are based on converting degrees to years of education using some standard length of education for each level of education. The resulting differences may partially reflect coding differences rather than real differences in length of education. More comparable numbers can be calculated from surveys that are conducted in a similar way in each country. Below we report numbers calculated from the International Adult Literacy Survey, where respondents in each country are asked about the total number of years spent in education over a lifetime.

Table 5.1
Level of education of the population
Average number of years of education for working-age population

	1970	1980	1990	2000	2004
Finland	8.6	9.6	10.4	11.2	11.2
Canada	11.4	12.1	12.5	13.0	13.2
Denmark	9.9	10.6	11.0	11.4	13.4
France	8.8	9.5	10.0	11.4	11.6
Germany	9.5	11.4	12.9	13.5	13.4
Italy	6.6	7.3	8.4	9.6	10.1
Japan	9.1	10.2	10.9	11.5	12.4
Netherlands	9.0	10.1	11.2	11.5	11.2
Norway	9.8	10.7	11.6	11.9	13.9
Sweden	9.1	10.1	11.1	12.7	12.6
United Kingdom	9.1	10.1	10.9	12.8	12.6
United States	11.6	12.2	12.6	13.6	13.3

Sources: OECD database and OECD Education at a Glance 2006.

The average educational level of the working-age population does not fully reveal the expansion of the Finnish educational system. Compared to many other countries, the expansion of the Finnish educational system occurred relatively late, and in 2000 there were still many workers who were educated in the 1960s. The average educational level continues to increase in Finland due to both the exit of older, less educated workers and the entry of young, better educated workers. As indicated in figure 5.3, the differences in educational levels across older and younger generations are very pronounced in Finland, indeed more so than in other Nordic countries, Germany, or the United States.

5.3 The Impact of Education on Productivity

A simple way to assess the effects of education on productivity is to weight the changes in employment of workers with different levels of education by their relative wages. If wage differences reflect differences in productivity, the difference between wage-weighted change in employment and the raw change in employment will reflect the increase in productivity due to the change in relative proportions of workers with different levels of education.

Below, we calculate the productivity contribution caused by the change in the composition of employment. In addition to grouping

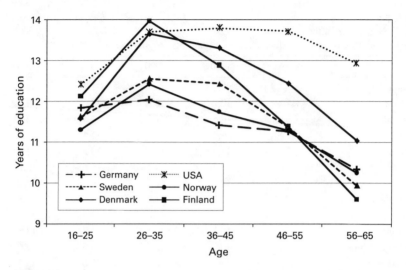

Figure 5.3
Average years of education by age group. *Source*: Own calculations from IALS data

workers according to education, we also group them by gender and age. Changes in the age structure, due to aging of the baby-boom cohorts, are noticeable as indicated in figure 5.4, and they also contribute to productivity growth. The share of the youngest cohorts in employment has declined because of both the decrease in cohort size and the rise in the age of entry to the labor market. The latter is due to increased time spent in education. The proportion of the oldest worker cohorts has grown mainly because the large cohorts that were born after the war have entered these cohorts, but also because participation rates among older cohorts have increased. Since older workers earn more than the young, our method of measuring productivity differences by relative wages indicates that aging has made a sizable contribution to productivity growth. An important caveat in these calculations is that there is evidence that wage differences do not always reflect productivity differences. For example, Ilmakunnas and Maliranta (2005) estimate plant-level production functions that include worker characteristics and show that wages increase with age more rapidly than does productivity. Evidence for the differential effects of education on wages and productivity is less conclusive.

Despite these concerns we proceed and illustrate the impact of the change in quality of labor on labor productivity for the period

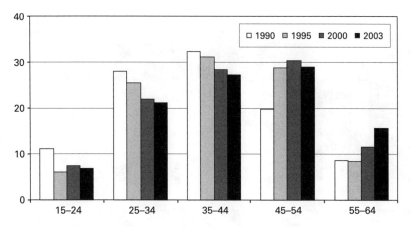

Figure 5.4
Employed by age. *Source*: Income Distribution Surveys, Statistics Finland

1990–2003 in figure 5.5. (We present the details of these productivity analyses in the appendix to this chapter.) According to the estimates, the quality-adjusted labor input has grown annually, on average, 0.3 percent more than raw employment. The estimates also show that the differences between change in raw employment and change in quality-adjusted employment were greatest when employment fell drastically between 1990 and 1993. The decrease in employment was more severe for the younger and less skilled employees. Therefore, the average productivity of the remaining employees increased significantly. When the employment rates started to rise in 1994, less productive workers were also able to find jobs and the quality change slowed down.

According to our calculations, the improvement in the quality of labor in Finland has had a significant impact on productivity growth. This result is in line with previous studies, even though the previous studies only examine the contribution of the change in educational level. For example, Elmeskov and Scarpetta (2000) calculate multifactor productivity (MFP) growth in twenty OECD countries between 1990 and 1998. They then adjust the estimates to account for changes in educational level. In Finland, the difference between these two estimates of MFP was among the highest in the OECD. Without the adjustment, the estimated average annual MFP growth was 3.2 percent. When the changes in human capital (measured by education) were accounted for, the estimate for MFP growth dropped to 2.8 percent, implying

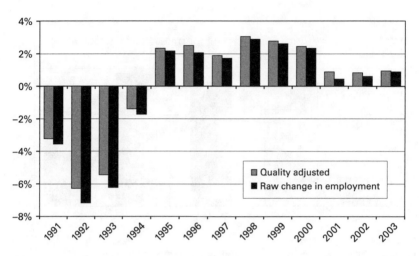

Figure 5.5
Effect of change in labor quality on productivity

that the improved educational level contributed almost half a percent-age point to the average annual MFP growth. Other countries where a comparable change took place were Italy and France. Elmeskov and Scarpetta (2000) note that in Italy and France (as in Finland), the change was largely due to a decline in employment of less skilled labor.

Moreover, Aulin-Ahmavaara (2000) estimates the effect of the change in educational level on labor productivity between 1990 and 1997 and finds that education accounted for 0.5 percent of average annual labor productivity growth. Also, according to these calculations the largest productivity effects of the change in educational level of employed workers occurred during the recession years 1991–1994.

5.4   Merits of the Finnish Educational System

We have shown that the Finnish educational system has expanded rap-idly in the past three decades and that the quantity of human capital, measured by average years of schooling, has increased more rapidly than in most other OECD countries.

Of course, as important as the quantity of education is its quality. The Finnish school system has performed extremely well in interna-tional quality comparisons. Finnish students have been among the top performers in the TIMMS study, which compares mathematics and

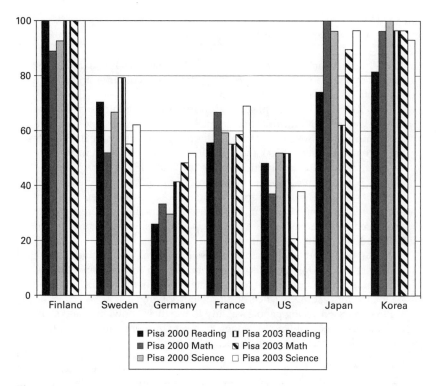

Figure 5.6
Education performance of Finnish 15-year-olds in international comparison. *Note*: Vertical axis gives the percentile ranking among participating OECD countries

science achievement. The younger cohorts of Finns also perform extremely well in the International Adult Literacy Survey, which measures literacy skills of the adult population. However, the performance of Finnish fifteen-year-olds in the international PISA study has received by far the most attention. In the first round of the PISA study, the Finnish students were best on the reading test of all forty-three participating countries. The Finnish students were also close to the top in math (fourth) and the sciences (third). In the second round of the PISA study in 2003, the Finnish students did even better: Finland had kept its lead in reading but was now at the top in the sciences and second to Hong Kong in mathematics. The results of the PISA studies are shown in figure 5.6, and box 5.1 provides some background on those studies.

High test scores could be the result of a high level of spending on schools or they could be an indication of high degrees of efficiency and productivity of the educational system. It turns out that investment in

Box 5.1
International tests of educational achievement

The Program for International Student Assessment (PISA) is an test battery that was jointly developed by participating countries and administered to fifteen-year-olds in schools.

The PISA study was implemented in forty-three countries in the first assessment in 2000, in forty-one countries in the second assessment in 2003, and in fifty-seven countries in the third assessment in 2006. Tests are given to between 4,500 and 10,000 students in each country. More than 0.4 million students participated in the 2006 PISA study.

Each participating student spent two hours carrying out pencil-and-paper tasks. Questions requiring students to construct their own answers were combined with multiple-choice items. Items were typically organized in units based on a written passage or graphic, of the kind that students might encounter in real life.

A total of six and a half hours of assessment items were included, with different students taking different combinations of the assessment items. Three and a half hours of the testing time was in mathematics, with one hour each for reading, science, and problem solving.

PISA assessed young people's ability to use their knowledge and skills in order to meet real-life challenges, rather than merely looking at how well they had mastered a specific school curriculum.

Source: Adapted from OECD 2000b.

---

human capital is not exceptionally high in Finland. Measured by share of GDP spent on education, Finland is close to the OECD average. This is illustrated by figure 5.7, which shows the GDP share of total public spending on educational institutions in selected countries.

In 1999 total expenditure on educational institutions from public and private sources for all levels of education was 5.8 percent of the GDP, exactly the same figure as for the OECD as a whole. In fact, expenditure on education as a share of the GDP decreased in Finland during the second half of the 1990s. This decline is partly explained by the rapid rise in GDP, because spending on education did not keep pace.

The success of Finnish students in the international assessments has aroused quite a bit interest in recent years. Some speculate that the explanation lies in the homogeneous student population. However, removing immigrants, for example, from the data used in comparisons has little effect on the results. Possible explanations also include remedial education for those with learning problems, discipline due to compulsory final exams and competition for places in higher education,

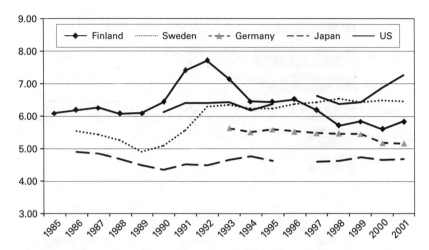

Figure 5.7
Total expenditure from public and private sources on educational institutions, % of GDP.
Source: OECD Education at a Glance Database: Education expenditures (2004)

and high teacher quality, with a university degree being required for all teachers. None of these explanations has been verified with convincing empirical studies, so the secret of Finland's success is still to be resolved.

Although the total expenditure on education in Finland is not exceptional by international standards, its allocation differs notably from most countries. The fraction of engineering graduates in tertiary education is the highest in Finland among the OECD countries, as indicated by figure 5.8.

Resources invested in engineering education may well have contributed to the success of the high-tech industries. The large number of new graduates has guaranteed a sufficient supply of engineers. A partial indicator of this is that, despite high growth rates in demand, the wages of engineers have not been very high in international comparison; see figure 5.9 for data on wages of electrical or mechanical engineers in different large cities. The wages of Finnish engineers are the lowest among the corresponding wages in the cities in figure 5.9.

Appendix 5.1: Measuring the Change in Labor Quality

A standard way to measure the growth of effective labor input is to weight the changes in employment in the different age and education

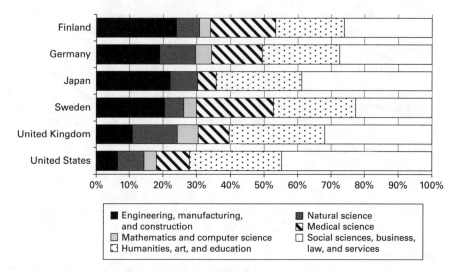

Figure 5.8
Graduates by field of study, 2000. *Source*: OECD, *Education at a Glance, OECD Indicators 2002*

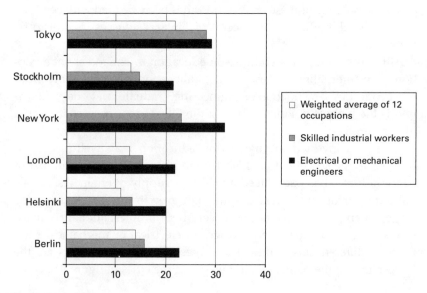

Figure 5.9
Gross income in U.S. dollars per hour, 2000. *Source*: Union Bank of Switzerland, Prices and Earnings Around the Globe, 2000 Edition

groups by their relative wage rates (Jorgenson, Gollop, and Fraumeni 1987). More precisely we can write

$$Log(L_t) - Log(L_{t-1}) = \sum_l \bar{v}_l[Log(L_{l,t}) - Log(L_{l,t-1})]$$

$$\bar{v}_l = \tfrac{1}{2}(v_{l,t} + v_{l,t-1})$$

$$v_l = \frac{p_l L_l}{\sum_l p_l L_l}$$

where $L_{l,t}$ is the labor input in group l, and p the average wage in each group. The growth of labor input is therefore a sum over increases in the type of labor input weighted by its value share, where the value share is calculated as an average over current and past periods.[1]

To calculate the growth of effective labor input we used data from the Income Distribution Survey for 1990 to 2003. The data contain information on earnings based on tax registers and months worked based on pension contributions. There is no working-hours information in the data, so the growth of labor input must be based on the growth in employment or the growth in months worked.

We limit the sample to individuals aged fifteen to sixty-four at the end of each year. We cross-classify the data into fifty groups by sex, five education categories, and five age groups. For each group we calculate the annual changes in (log) employment and (log) months worked. The value share weights are calculated by dividing the earnings of each group by total earnings in each year. We include both wages and salaries and entrepreneurial income in our earnings measure and use annual figures as reported in tax filings to calculate the earnings shares.

We cannot directly calculate the changes in hours worked by different types of labor because hours of work are not included in the Income Distribution Survey. However, we can compare hours worked in some main categories to employment growth in the Labor Force Survey to assess the magnitude of the bias. While the aggregate changes appear to be close, there are some differences. The largest differences are that the months in employment appear to decrease more slowly at the onset of the recession in 1991 than does employment in the sample and in the National Accounts. Also, the high employment growth in 1994 appears not to be in line with the National Accounts.

6   The New Economy in Finland

Since the mid-1990s Finland has been heralded as a successful model for rapid structural change and for the introduction of what is called the "New Economy."[1] In this chapter we first discuss research and development (R&D) in general, after which we focus on the rapid rise of the information and communication technology (ICT) industry. This is because the huge structural changes in the Finnish economy were indeed largely concentrated in the ICT industry.

In discussing the rise of ICT we pay particular attention to the phenomenal success of one company, the Nokia Group. However, the Finnish story is not only about Nokia, so we look at the development and role of the larger Finnish ICT industry both over time and in comparison with some other countries. After this background, we consider the "Nokia case" in some detail.

6.1   Research and Development

As we have seen in chapter 5, the multifactor productivity growth was a main driver of output growth in Finland during the past decade. Since R&D spending can be seen as an investment in innovation, it is important to examine its level and development.

Figure 6.1 shows that total R&D spending in Finland (as a percent of GDP) increased significantly in the 1990s, as it also has in recent years, in line with developments in the Nordic countries (except Norway). It reached the second highest level in the OECD area, with only Sweden spending more on R&D. These numbers show that during the 1990s Finland became a country with high R&D spending, in conformity with our general argument about its rapid transformation into a high-tech economy.

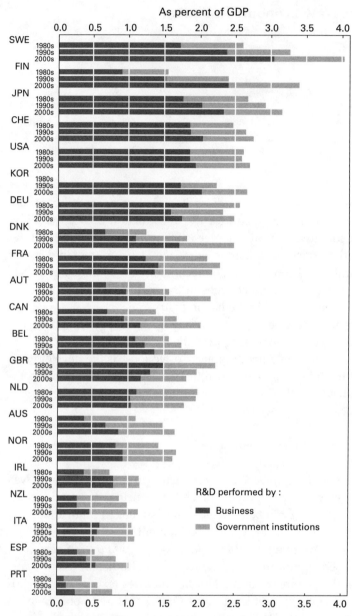

Figure 6.1
R & D spending in international comparison. *Source*: OECD

While in Finland the increase in overall R&D expenditure reflected increases in both business R&D and government R&D, in many other countries government R&D declined in the 1990s as a percent of GDP, reflecting a reduction in military spending and efforts to reduce fiscal deficits. It should be noted that the increase in government spending on R&D in Finland was not focused on military R&D.

To the best of our knowledge there is no study available on the impact of R&D spending on growth in Finland, but OECD estimates suggest that in general a 10 percent increase in business R&D intensity (about 0.1 percent of GDP) boosts annual GDP growth by 0.3 to 0.4 percentage points. This could imply a long-run effect on the level of GDP per capita of about 1.2 percent under the conservative assumption that changes in R&D do not permanently affect output growth but raise GDP per capita to a higher level, so that the impact of growth is only temporary until this higher income level is reached (see chapter 2 in OECD 2003b). According to endogenous growth theory, which claims that R&D activity raises the growth rate permanently, the overall effect on the level of GDP would be much larger, pointing to significant externalities for R&D. The empirical results regarding the effects of nonbusiness (including government) R&D are not so clear. The reason may be that this R&D spending, used for defense purposes, fundamental science, and health, may generate basic knowledge with possible technology spillovers in the longer run. But in growth regressions, such effects are difficult to identify given the long time lags involved.

A number of investigators have examined the significance of R&D for economic growth. Griffith, Redding, and Van Reenen (2004), Zachariadis (2006), and Aiginger and Falk (2005) also provide recent statistically significant evidence of the effects of R&D on productivity and output growth using data from OECD countries, including Finland. Ali-Yrkkö and Maliranta (2006) analyze the productivity impact of R&D using a large panel data set for Finnish firms over the period 1996–2004. For the short run (one to two years), they do not find any statistically significant productivity impact of R&D. However, R&D does have an economically and statistically significant impact when one takes into account R&D efforts of three to five years earlier. Hence, there is a significant lag between R&D and its positive outcome for productivity. Ali-Yrkkö (2005) examines the impact of public R&D financing on labor demand using Finnish panel data for the period

Table 6.1
Shares of ICT industries in value added of market sector

	1985	1990	1995	2000	2003
Manufacture of electrical and optical equipment (sectors 31–32)	1.3	1.7	2.6	6.1	5.2
Telecommunication services (sector 64)	2.2	2.2	2.2	3.2	3.6
Computer software and services (sector 72)	0.7	0.8	1.9	1.6	1.9
Total ICT	4.2	4.7	5.7	10.9	10.6

Note: Sector numbering follows the Groningen database.
Source: Our calculations using the Groningen database, http://www.ggdc.net/dseries/60-industry.html.

1997–2002 and shows that the public financing increases R&D employment.

6.2   The High-Technology Industry in Finland

We will focus on the Finnish ICT industry, which is often referred to as the New Economy. High technology in Finland is currently dominated by ICT even if Finland also invests in other areas of high technology—notably in the biosciences, which have not yet had a major commercial impact.[2] It should also be noted that high technology is not just manufacturing of ICT commodities such as cellular phones. High technology is very much a part of the more traditional industries, so that in looking at the role of ICT it is important to distinguish between ICT in different industries—that is, between the use of ICT in traditional production processes and the production of ICT commodities.

6.2.1   ICT Developments in Finland

A common way to examine the impact of the ICT industry is to measure its contribution to the growth of aggregate output and its share of the value added of the business sector. We begin by considering the share of ICT industries in the market sector. The results in table 6.1 show that this share has grown gradually over time, though the most recent years show a leveling off from the peak of the ICT boom. In the period 1980–2003 the ICT share of value added has risen from 4.2 percent in 1980 to 10.6 percent in 2003. The increase was particularly rapid in the second half of 1990s.

Next, we look at the role of ICT in economic growth using a standard growth-accounting framework. See the appendix for a classifica-

Table 6.2
Average growth contribution of ICT industries to GDP, 1995–2005

	1995–2005
Output growth, %	4.1
Contribution from ICT industries, percentage points	0.9

Source: Jalava and Pohjola 2007.

tion scheme for assessing the ICT contribution to economic growth using the growth-accounting approach. Table 6.2, which is adapted from Jalava and Pohjola 2007, shows that the ICT industry contributed nearly a third of total economic growth in the period 1995–2002.

A different question concerns the role of ICT in the growth process of the overall economy. Looking first at the stock of ICT capital, its role can be measured in different ways. The ICT share of the Finnish productive nonresidential capital stock has been estimated at over 9 percent in 1999, up from about 4 percent in 1985, according to Jalava and Pohjola 2002. Another tack is to consider the role of ICT in growth of output. Estimates of the contribution of ICT to real output growth are presented in table 6.3.[3]

Table 6.3 shows that, in the second half of the 1990s and the beginning of the 2000s, the contribution of ICT capital to output growth was much higher than the contributions of other forms of capital. A similar picture emerges for growth in labor productivity, whereas in multifactor productivity growth the role of other factors is clearly greater than that of ICT. Overall, ITC contributed about a quarter of the average annual output growth of about 4 percent over the 1995–2002 period.

According to the longer-term data in Jalava and Pohjola 2002, the contribution of ICT capital to output has increased steadily (along with labor quality and multifactor productivity), while the contributions of other factors of production have not shown much systematic increase. The results of Jalava and Pohjola 2002, 2007, also include a surprise: growth in labor productivity has slowed somewhat since the second half of the 1990s despite the increasing role of ICT. This result is due to negative contributions from other forms of capital. This last development contrasts with that in the United States, where labor productivity has been growing as a result of an expanding employment share in the ICT production sector and faster productivity growth in the service industries that make intensive use of ICT (see, e.g., van Ark et al. 2003).[4]

Table 6.3
Contributions to real output growth and to labor productivity in GDP, 1995–2005

I. Output growth		4.06	
Contributions from	ICT capital	0.50	
	Other capital	0.32	
	Dwellings	0.25	
	Labor services	0.92	
	Multifactor productivity	2.07	
Growth rates	ICT capital	15.14	
	Other capital	1.51	
	Dwellings	2.34	
	Labor services	1.41	
II. Labor productivity growth		2.87	
Contributions from			
Capital deepening		0.66	
	ICT capital		0.46
	Other capital		0.07
	Dwellings		0.13
Labor quality		0.14	
Multifactor productivity*		2.07	
	ICT related		1.41
	Other		0.66

*The breakdown of multifactor productivity is computed by estimating MFP growth in ICT production and in other areas of production and weighting those estimates according to the weights in direct output contributions.
Source: Jalava and Pohjola 2007.

6.2.2   Finnish ICT in International Comparison

We start by comparing the role of ICT capital in Finland and selected other countries using the growth-accounting framework. Table 6.4 gives the results for EU countries with a large role of ICT and for the United States as a basis of comparison.[5]

Table 6.4 gives the results of growth-accounting calculations for EU countries for which the high-technology sector has had the biggest impact on economic growth, and also for the United States as a benchmark. It can be seen that the growth contribution of ICT in Finland is comparable to that of Ireland, Sweden, and the United Kingdom, which are the EU countries with major growth contributions from ICT capital (see chapter 6 of EEAG 2006). In the second half of the 1990s, ICT capital contributed about 0.6–0.8 percentage points to aggregate

Table 6.4
Growth accounting for selected countries*

	GDP growth	Contributions to GDP growth by			
		ICT capital growth	Non-ICT capital growth	Labor growth	TFP growth
Ireland					
1995–2000	9.7	0.6	2.3	2.1	4.7
2000–2004	5.0	0.4	2.3	0.5	1.9
Finland					
1995–2000	4.9	0.7	0.1	1.0	3.0
2000–2004	2.3	0.6	0.3	−0.3	1.7
Sweden					
1995–2000	3.5	0.8	0.4	0.7	1.7
2000–2004	2.1	0.4	0.2	−0.4	1.9
UK					
1995–2000	3.3	0.8	0.6	0.7	1.2
2000–2004	2.3	0.34	0.5	0.2	1.3
United States					
1995–2000	4.2	0.9	0.6	1.3	1.5
2000–2004	2.4	0.6	0.4	−0.3	1.7

Note: Columns in growth-accounting tables may not add because of rounding.
*The results are adapted from chapter 3 of EEAG 2006.
Source: Adapted from EEAG 2006.

growth, though the contribution fell somewhat in the period 2000–2004, when the big boom in ICT was over. It is also clear that the role of ICT in these EU countries was similar to its growth role in the U.S. economy.[6]

Table 6.5 shows the developments in various types of ICT investment during the 1990s in international comparison.[7] In comparing EU countries, it can be observed that, in the first half of the decade, Ireland, Denmark, Great Britain, Sweden, and Finland were conspicuous as countries in which ICT investment grew more rapidly than the European average. Correspondingly, Austria, Germany, Italy, and Portugal stayed below the EU average.

There are also big differences between EU countries in terms of different types of ICT investment. In the first half of the 1990s, of the countries that exhibited rapid growth, Ireland concentrated on office and computer equipment, Finland on communication equipment, and

Table 6.5
Growth in ICT Investments in EU countries and the United States, 1990–1995 and 1996–2000

	Office and computer equipment		Communication equipment		Software		Entire ICT sector	
	1990–1995	1995–2000	1990–1995	1995–2000	1990–1995	1995–2000	1990–1995	1995–2000
Austria	11.2	32.9	2.6	10.0	8.1	17.8	5.9	17.9
Denmark	14.8	26.0	−0.5	8.2	16.6	14.5	13.6	16.7
Finland	16.9	28.6	25.2	26.1	4.8	13.0	9.2	18.4
France	12.9	30.2	3.9	10.2	6.7	17.7	7.9	19.0
Germany	8.8	33.9	1.9	12.0	7.4	11.4	5.9	19.4
Ireland	38.7	34.6	6.2	19.4	8.4	22.3	21.4	27.1
Italy	7.7	33.1	5.5	11.9	4.2	11.4	5.6	16.6
Holland	13.1	30.5	1.8	15.3	4.5	19.1	7.4	22.3
Portugal	10.4	31.9	2.7	12.2	8.7	13.2	6.1	17.2
Spain	1.6	30.1	−0.2	13.5	−2.3	11.1	−0.2	18.2
Sweden	15.8	26.8	15.8	13.8	10.9	16.5	12.6	17.6
UK	13.5	30.4	15.6	10.4	11.5	17.3	12.8	17.3
EU	10.7	31.6	4.6	11.9	7.6	18.5	7.7	18.5
United States	17.4	27.0	4.1	15.7	10.1	19.3	11.0	19.3

Source: van Ark et al. 2003.

Denmark on software investment. Sweden and Great Britain proceeded on a broader front: in those countries, ICT investment grew rapidly in all sectors.

In the second half of the 1990s, ICT investment increased rapidly in many EU countries while the differences between these countries narrowed. On the whole, in the second half of the decade Finland remained close to the EU average, and ICT investment continued to be targeted specifically at the communication-equipment sector. Table 6.5 also shows that in the first half of the decade ICT investment in the United States rose more rapidly than in the European Union, whereas the difference was smaller in the second half of the decade, as growth of ICT investment accelerated in both the European Union and the United States.

A different measure of the importance of ICT is obtained when ICT investment is related to total investment. Table 6.6 presents the share of ICT investment in total fixed capital formation in the period 1980–

Table 6.6
ICT investment as share of Gross Fixed Capital Formation, %

	1980	1985	1990	1995	2000
UK	5.6	11.0	13.8	20.9	22.0
Sweden	5.0	8.7	9.7	15.8	21.6
Netherlands	11.2	14.6	15.5	16.4	20.9
Germany	7.7	13.9	13.9	13.9	19.2
Denmark	6.4	9.0	11.1	16.1	19.1
Finland	3.9	5.5	7.0	14.2	17.5
Italy	8.0	12.5	8.3	16.0	14.6
Ireland	4.6	12.3	8.3	16.0	14.6
France	6.1	9.5	8.5	9.9	13.1
Austria	7.1	9.6	10.0	10.4	12.8
Portugal	6.1	11.9	10.6	11.5	11.4
Spain	5.6	9.4	11.9	9.3	10.1
EU	7.1	11.6	12.2	14.1	17.1
United States	15.5	21.3	22.8	25.6	29.6

Source: van Ark et al. 2003.

2000 in different European countries, as well as in the European Union and the United States. In 1995 and 2000 the shares of ICT in EU countries range from a high share of about 21 percent to a low share of about 10 percent.

Finland's ICT investment as a percentage of total investment (fixed capital formation) is somewhat higher than the EU average.[8] This is the result of a big increase during the 1990s. Before that time, Finland's share of ICT investment in total investment was below the EU average. Moreover, the increase in the ICT share in 1990–2000 was the second highest in the EU; only in Sweden was the increase larger. The rise of ICT was more gradual in some other European countries with a large share of ICT investment. The United Kingdom, the Netherlands, and Germany provide examples of more gradual rises. By comparison, the share of ICT in the United States also increased moderately during the period. But because the share was already very high in 1980, by 2000 ICT investment as a share of total investment remained much higher than in any European country.

Looking at the structure of the ICT sector, Finland has a relatively high share in manufacturing of ICT commodities; see table 6.1. This feature is shared with Far East countries like Japan and South Korea.

In contrast, the Finnish share of ICT services is comparable to that in many other countries, while the share of telecommunications is relatively low (see Haltiwanger and Jarmin 2003, figure 2; Rouvinen and Ylä-Anttila 2003).

Daveri (2002; see his table 2) compares the role of ICT in raising labor productivity and suggests surprisingly that ICT did not boost productivity very much in the EU countries during the 1990s. Growth in labor productivity in the "high-ICT" countries has been slower than in the "low-ICT" adopters, leading in the aggregate to negative productivity growth per employed person in the EU.[9] In contrast, in the United States the increase in labor productivity has been positive. This fact is partly explained by other factors that have constrained productivity growth, but even if the other factors are eliminated, the ICT contribution remains at the low end. For Finland the picture is somewhat better in the sense that the ICT contribution to growth has been among the highest in Western European EU countries (see Daveri 2002, table 3). Indeed, looking at changes in levels of labor productivity in Finnish industry, it appears that Finland has caught up to the United States and may even have surpassed it (see the figures in Koski, Rouvinen, and Ylä-Anttila 2002, 42).

An interesting aspect of the Finnish economy is the high share of mergers and acquisitions relative to other countries. Finland tops the list of EU countries in the share of mergers and acquisitions within the EU countries during the period 1991–1999 and ranks second among EU countries in share of foreign mergers and acquisitions relative to the size of the economy.[10] This data suggests that industrial dynamics have been rapid in Finland, and there is also evidence that much of the merger-and-acquisition activity has been in the Finnish ICT sector (see Pajarinen and Ylä-Anttila 2001).

Finally, we compare Finland to other selected countries in terms of the size and diffusion of ICT.

Table 6.7 shows that Finland is one of the leading countries in terms of ICT production. This fact also translates into a high level of foreign trade in communication goods, where in 1998 Finland was a world leader in per-capita ICT trade surplus (USD 1000), with Sweden (USD 800) and Ireland (USD 200) ranking second and third according to this measure.[11] Yet, it should be noted that production of ICT goods and services is not the only measure of the role of ICT in Finland. The use of ICT in other parts of the economy (diffusion of ICT) is at least an equally important part of the New Economy. Diffusion can be mea-

Table 6.7
Share of ICT industry in value added of market sector, selected countries

	1990	1995	2000	2003
Finland	4.7	5.7	10.9	10.6
Sweden	4.5	5.4	7.1	6.0
EU-15	5.3	5.1	6.0	5.7
United States	5.6	6.3	7.2	6.2

Source: Our calculations using the Groningen data, http://www.ggdc.net/dseries/ 60-industry.html.

Table 6.8
ICT spending in Finland, Sweden, and the United States, % of GDP

Year	Finland	Sweden	EU	United States
2004	7.1	8.7	6.5	7.8
2003	7.0	8.8	6.4	7.9

Source: Eurostat.

sured with various indicators. Perhaps the most direct measure is spending on ICT goods and services (defined as IT and telecommunication goods and services). The results for this indicator are shown in table 6.8.

Finland does not head the list by this measure but is among the better performers in Europe. Table 6.8 shows that in 2001 the share of ICT spending per GDP for Finland was above the EU average but below the U.S. figure. Finland is also well below Sweden, which is a world leader in ICT according to this indicator. This picture is similar to that obtained by looking at other broader indicators like use of the Internet or personal computers per capita. For example, in 2003 there were 534 Internet users per 1,000 people in Finland, slightly fewer than the 573 users for Sweden and 551 for the United States. In mobile phone subscribers in 2004 there were 96 users per 100 people in Finland, which can be compared to 108 subscribers in Sweden and 62 in the United States. Overall, we conclude that Finland is among the high performers in ICT diffusion but not quite number one.[12]

How should Finland be assessed overall in terms of ICT activities relative to other developed countries? We can conclude from the international comparison that during the 1990s, the Finnish economy became a high-tech economy. This is particularly true in terms of measures of ICT production, at which Finland excels. However, a standard measure of ICT diffusion gives a somewhat different picture: Finland is not quite at the forefront in the use of ICT but is among the top performers, especially in comparison with the EU-15 countries. Overall, one can say that Finland appears to have some scope for improvement in the use of ICT in different parts of the economy.

6.3   The Nokia Case

As is well known, the Nokia Group has dominated the high-tech sector in Finland.[13] Nokia is an unusually large firm for a small country like Finland. Nokia is the leading producer of mobile phones in the world, with a market share of about 30 percent in 2004 and above 35 percent in most recent years. In the mid-1990s its market share was just over 20 percent, and it rose to about 35 percent in the year 2000. Nokia is also a large supplier of networks for mobile phones, and in networks it is the second largest producer after Ericsson. Networks account for about a quarter of its net sales.[14]

The size of Nokia relative to the Finnish economy and society can be described by various measures. Nokia's R&D spending in 2001 was close to a third of total R&D spending in Finland and nearly half of the private-sector R&D. With R&D spending of foreign affiliates included, in 2001 Nokia spent about EUR 3 billion, while total R&D spending in Finland was about EUR 3.5 billion. In the high-growth period toward the end of the 1990s Nokia grew very rapidly and, for example, in 2000 at the peak of the ICT boom, it was estimated to account for 2.8 percent of Finnish GDP and contributed over 1.6 percentage points of its annual growth.

While Nokia has had a major impact on Finnish economic growth, exports, and R&D activities, its direct impact on employment has been much smaller. In 2001 Nokia had nearly 24,000 employees in Finland, which is about 2 percent of total employees in the business sector. About 60 percent of its Finnish staff (and one-third of its total staff) works in R&D. In 2001 Nokia paid EUR 0.7 billion in taxes in Finland, which is about 2 percent of general government tax revenues.

These impressive numbers are the outcome of phenomenal success in the 1990s. The Nokia story is exciting, and we give a brief sketch of it in the following paragraphs. The Nokia case is also interesting in that, as discussed below, it raises questions about the role of government and its technology policy in creating industrial successes.

6.3.1   A Brief History of Nokia

Nokia is the outgrowth of mergers between different companies, the oldest of which was established in 1865.[15] Officially, the current limited company Nokia was created in 1967, through a merger between a firm that, among other things, produced cables and metal products and another that produced rubber products. The Nokia of the 1980s could be described as a conglomerate of a variety of different divisions producing very different kinds of commodities, ranging from forestry, metal products, cables, and tires to consumer electronics (especially TVs). Mobile phones were only a small (but growing) business for Nokia in the mid-1980s.

The 1980s were very turbulent times for Nokia. The management expanded the company aggressively via the acquisition of other firms, thereby opening new production lines. Some of these acquisitions turned out to be disastrous, of which the purchase of several TV production firms in central Europe was the biggest failure. The structure of Nokia's ownership created another difficulty that became acute in the second half of the 1980s. At that time the Finnish financial system was very much bank centered, and the two biggest Finnish commercial banks were both large owners of Nokia. With the deregulation and increased competition in the Finnish financial system, these two banks became major rivals and wanted to give up ownership in Nokia. Eventually, one of them (Kansallis-osakepankki, which ceased to exist after the merger with the other commercial bank in 1995) sold its shares in Nokia and the ownership structure was revised at the end of 1991. The visible and severe feuds among top management—a third major problem at Nokia—were resolved at the beginning of 1992. Together with adverse aggregate developments in Finland and other countries (discussed in chapters 2 and 3), these difficulties meant that Nokia faced serious challenges in the early 1990s. Many of its major divisions were in deep trouble. The mobile phone and telecommunication divisions were profitable, but at the end of the 1980s they were a relatively small part of Nokia's total business activity (only 17 percent of total turnover in 1989).

The ownership arrangements and the new management were a major factor in Nokia's new strategy, launched at the beginning of the 1990s. The core of the new strategy was a concentration on ICT, especially those areas where growth and good profitability were perceived to be possible. Traditional businesses were sold: tires and forestry in

Table 6.9
Performance indicators for Nokia 1996–2000, EUR million at 2000 prices

	1996	1997	1998	1999	2000
Turnover	7076	9380	13992	20365	30376
Profits before taxes	768	1597	2613	4025	5776
Stock market value (end of year)	13595	19613	61590	215652	222876
Return on equity (%)	22.7	38.3	50.2	55.7	58.0
Indebtedness (%)	−9	−35	−36	−41	−26

Source: Häikiö 2001, part III.

1988–1991, cables and metals in 1994–1996, and—after hard restructuring and much effort—consumer electronics in 1996. The restructuring and the success in ICT led to a turnaround in Nokia's profitability. In 1991 the company posted losses (EUR 19 million in year 2000 money value) and the return on equity was a scant 3.4 percent. Three years later, in 1994, profits had soared to 659 million and the rate of return had risen to 25.4 percent. The key factor in this rapid growth was the introduction of the GSM standard in mobile phones. GSM was universally adopted in European countries and many other countries as well, with the United States and Japan holding out as the major exceptions. GSM was later introduced in the United States.

The dramatic turnaround was sustained through the 1990s, and the company became both very big and highly profitable. Table 6.9 provides data on the development of Nokia over the period 1996–2000 when it grew apace.

Nokia's extremely rapid growth necessitated reforms in its mode of operation. In particular, new production and logistical arrangements were introduced to meet the rapid growth in mobile phones and networks. Continuous product improvements were also made and, for example, the Internet revolution came to mobile phones as well in the late 1990s. New product developments continue in the mobile phone business, and the next stages in the ICT business appear to lie in linking mobile communications more and more closely with the Internet. However, the growth boom of the mobile phone business seems to be over at least for the time being.

In figure 6.2 we present stock-price comparisons between Nokia, Ericsson, and Motorola over the period 1995–2004. (The data has been converted to indexes with 1995 equal to 100.) As the figure shows, there has been much volatility, especially in the share prices of Nokia and Ericsson, but much less so in the share price of Motorola. More-

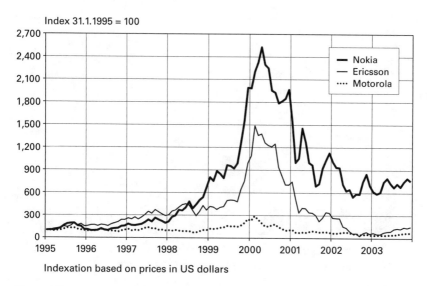

Figure 6.2
Stock price comparison. *Source*: Bloomberg

over, Nokia's stock price has been higher than the prices of the other two since mid-1998. Nokia's price rose rapidly in the stock market boom of the 1990s; while the end of the boom brought a decline in the price, it still remained at a higher level than the prices of Ericsson and Motorola. As we have already noted, Nokia is presently the market leader in mobile phones, and it also has a large market share in the supporting networks.

Figure 6.3 describes price per earnings over the period 1995–2004 for Nokia, Ericsson, and Motorola. The period is marked by gyrations in this index as well, and during the last few years Nokia's P/E index has dropped to a relatively low level.[16]

6.3.2 Why Did Nokia Succeed?

Looking at the history of ICT at Nokia, one sees its roots in the 1960s when a small electronics unit was launched to develop specific products, first for military and then for civilian use. Telephone switching equipment and radiophones were major products with which Nokia was very successful. Radiophones were first produced for military use, but civilian uses were also envisioned. A major milestone was the common Nordic NMT standard for mobile phones in the early 1980s. At that time it was the largest such network in the world and also the

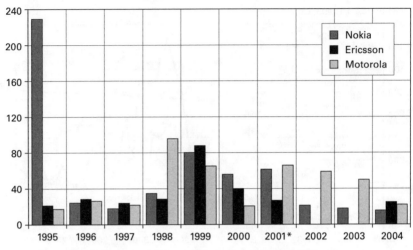

* Ericsson's data from 30.6.2001 and Motorola's from 30.9.2001

Figure 6.3
P/E-ratio

most advanced technologically. The introduction of NMT fostered development of a variety of ICT products: phones, networks, support stations, and so on. Not only did the companies take part in the development of ICT products but the telephone operators did as well, which accelerated the adoption of the new products. This process laid the groundwork for engineering know-how, and in a way the Nordic countries were a test ground for new products and product development.

Engineering know-how was naturally also abetted by the supply of good engineers; the availability of qualified personnel in Finland was long a critical factor for Nokia. Finnish recruitment remained the main source of new personnel through much of the 1990s until about 1998 (see Ollila 2000). After that, Nokia could no longer rely exclusively on Finnish resources, because the company had grown so large.

An important question to address is the following: What degree of Nokia's success can be attributed to its own actions and what degree to its favorable operating environment? Of course, a precise assessment of factors cannot be done here, but in what follows we sketch a general explanation.

Some credit for the success of Nokia and ICT in Finland can be ascribed to wise government policies. First, the role of the governments in the Nordic countries was important, because their decisions made the adoption of the common NMT standard possible even if the huge success only came later with the introduction of the GSM standard. Second, the supply of highly skilled engineers and scientists was to a large extent provided by the Finnish higher education system, which has consistently laid heavy emphasis on engineering, as discussed in chapter 5. Third, the government has provided significant public support for Nokia's R&D through the National Technology Agency (TEKES). Over the years the TEKES support for Nokia has varied a great deal, but it has been considered quite significant, especially in the 1980s and early 1990s (see Ali-Yrkkö and Hermans 2002 for details). In recent years, public support has diminished relative to the size of Nokia. In 1991 the TEKES support was 10 percent of Nokia's R&D expenditure, whereas in 2004 it amounted to only 0.4 percent of R&D.

The main reasons for Nokia's success are naturally internal to the company, although government support and the promotion of engineering education have played an important complementary role. Nokia's flexible, nonhierarchical management is a major factor in its excellent results against a backdrop of admittedly favorable prospects of the mobile phone industry. It should be kept in mind that in the 1990s Nokia was relatively much more successful than its major competitors, Ericsson and Motorola, in the ICT business. That success was made possible in large part by internal business creativity.[17] Nokia was quick to introduce new add-on products, designed for the consumer mass market. A wide range of changeable phone covers in different colors and patterns is just one example of flexible product design for different types of consumers. Naturally, luck has also played a part; it is impossible to have such success if the market opportunities do not exist (see Ollila 2000).

There is no doubt that since the 1990s Nokia has been very important for the Finnish economy in the aggregate, as the data we have provided show. The contribution of Nokia to the GDP and other macrovariables do not, however, tell the whole story. First, Nokia has an extensive network of suppliers of parts and components for its products. Second, its R&D efforts have facilitated the rise of other new ICT firms, especially in software, and it also cooperates with Finnish universities (mostly in engineering and technology). The links between Nokia and other areas of the Finnish ICT industry appear significant at least in qualitative terms (see, e.g., Ali-Yrkkö 2001), although quantitative evidence provided by Daveri and Silva (2004) casts some doubt on the strength of the spillover effects and linkages from Nokia to other Finnish ICT firms in communication manufacturing, telecommunication and business services, and computers. Using input-output tables, Daveri and Silva (2004) find that, though the linkages exist, they appear relatively small in quantitative terms. The limited linkages between ICT industries and Nokia in input-output terms reflect to a large extent features that are typical of a small, open economy. Firms that are very big relative to the domestic economy must rely on imported factors of production, and they also export most of their output.

Appendix 6.1: Growth Accounting for ICT Capital

A common framework for assessing ICT contribution to growth is the growth-accounting approach (see, e.g., Colecchia and Schreyer 2002, Daveri 2003, Jalava and Pohjola 2002, 2007, and Stiroh 2004). This approach assumes that aggregate output in the market sector is given by the production function

$$Y(Y_{ICT}, Y_O) = AF(K_{ICT}, K_O, L),$$

where Y, Y_{ICT}, Y_O are value added of aggregate output, ICT goods, and other goods, respectively. Correspondingly, A, K_{ICT}, K_O, L are multifactor productivity, ICT capital services, other capital services, and labor services. Under constant returns to scale in production and perfect competition, the share-weighted growth of output is equal to the sum of share-weighted growths of inputs and multifactor productivity, so that growth can be expressed as

$$\hat{Y} = w_{ICT}\hat{Y}_{ICT} + w_O\hat{Y}_O = v_{ICT}\hat{K}_{ICT} + v_O\hat{K}_O + v_L\hat{L} + \hat{A},$$

where ˆ denotes rate of change, w_{ICT} and w_O are nominal output shares, and v_{ICT}, v_O, v_L are nominal income shares of the inputs, so that $v_{ICT} + v_O + v_L = 1$ under constant returns to scale.

7   Remaining Policy Challenges

Since the crisis in the first half of the 1990s the Finnish economy has largely performed well, especially as compared to most Western European countries. The relative economic success of Finland should, however, not mask the problems it must face now and in the foreseeable future. In this concluding chapter we consider the remaining legacies from the 1990s and the primary challenges that lie ahead for Finland.

The three main challenges the Finnish economy continues to face are (1) persistently high unemployment, (2) the rapid aging of the population, and (3) pressures from the globalization process on the location of production activities, the labor market, and public finances. Of course, Finland is not the only country facing these problems. Most other Western European economies are struggling with exactly the same concerns.[1]

7.1   The Unemployment Problem

As discussed earlier, the economic crisis in the early 1990s led to a huge increase in unemployment. Given the extent of the crisis, the rapid increase in unemployment was not surprising. The challenge lies in the relatively slow rate of decline in unemployment despite rapid economic growth since the mid-1990s. Various factors appear to have contributed to the rise in structural unemployment and also to the withdrawal of specific groups of the population from the labor market. While a good part of this development was related to the crisis of the early 1990s, the fact that the decline in the utilization of labor potential has not subsequently been fully reversed points to the importance of major structural factors that are reducing the functioning of the labor market.

Despite the resumption of fast economic growth in 1994, the unemployment rate decreased only gradually, and it currently remains at a high level, near the EU average (see figure 1.2 in chapter 1). To the extent that unemployment results from structural malfunctions, attempts to reduce unemployment via growth-enhancing fiscal and monetary policies are bound to fail, possibly resulting only in higher inflation.[2]

We can begin with the structural change in the Finnish economy in the 1990s. During the four years of economic crisis, 1990–1994, roughly 450,000 jobs were lost and total employment declined by 18 percent from its 1990 level. In the first quarter of 1994, employment was slightly below two million, which was at the lowest level since 1949. Since 1994, employment has grown steadily, by approximately 2 percent per year. By 2001, total employment had grown by 313,000, or by about two-thirds of the decline in the early 1990s.

During the recession some sectors suffered much more than others. The construction industry was hit particularly hard; in fact, half of the jobs in construction disappeared between 1990 and 1994. Employment also declined by approximately 25 percent in various other job sectors, including parts of manufacturing, retail trade, hotels and restaurants, and financial services.

In the recovery after 1994, the largest increases in employment occurred in business services and in equipment manufacturing. The electronics industry was responsible for most of the growth in manufacturing; other manufacturing sectors experienced only modest increases in employment. The service sector, particularly business services, education, and social services, grew rapidly. The newly created jobs were quite different from the jobs lost in the early 1990s. The fastest-growing service sectors had only experienced small employment declines during the recession. Of the sectors that experienced large job losses during the recession, employment returned close to the prerecession level only in equipment manufacturing. Less than half of the employment decline in construction and only a third of the employment decline in retail trade were matched by employment growth after 1994.

Another way to describe the structural change is to examine changes in the occupational structure. In figure 7.1 we compare the changes in employment by occupation over the 1990s using data from the Income Distribution Survey. In the figure the occupations are ordered according to average wage in 1990 and grouped into deciles on the horizontal axis. The vertical axis gives the changes in employment in each group

Figure 7.1
Employment change by occupation, 1990–2000. *Source*: Own calculations based on data from Finnish Income Distribution Survey

of occupations. As figure 7.1 shows, employment growth was concentrated in the high-wage occupations. Simultaneously, average employment declined, the decline being particularly severe in the low-wage occupations.

The rapid structural change in employment created an increasing mismatch problem in the labor market. Unemployed former construction workers were poorly equipped to find jobs in the growing service sector. Since those jobs often demanded a higher educational level than the unemployed possessed, the differences in unemployment rates across groups with different levels of education grew rapidly. In the mid-1990s the unemployment rate for workers with only basic compulsory education exceeded 20 percent, while that for university graduates remained around 3–4 percent. Uneven regional development also contributed to the mismatch problem. After the recession, employment growth was rapid in the capital (Helsinki) region and Southern Finland and much slower in the high-unemployment regions in Northern and Eastern Finland (see Koskela and Uusitalo 2006).

The clearest indication of a growing mismatch is given by the Beveridge curve, showing the relationship between unemployment rate and

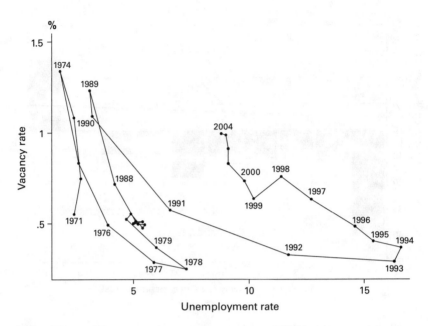

Figure 7.2
Beveridge curve for Finland. *Source*: *Finnish Labor Review* 2/2005

open vacancies in the employment offices. Figure 7.2 displays the Beveridge curve for the period 1971–2004. It shows how most of the variation in unemployment rate is related to the business cycle (movements from northwest to southeast along the curve). However, the curve has also moved outward in two definite shifts. The first occurred in the late 1970s and the other, much larger, took place in the early 1990s. By the year 2000, the vacancy rate was back to its 1988 level, but the unemployment rate was about 6 percentage points higher. More recently, in 2001–2004, the vacancy rate increased, but the unemployment rate declined only slightly.

For most of the 1980s, long-term unemployment was not much of a problem in Finland. The average duration of unemployment spells was around twenty-four weeks, and the proportion of the long-term unemployed (unemployed for more than a year) was slightly over 10 percent. This favorable picture changed during the depression in the early 1990s. By 1995 almost a third of the unemployed were classified as long-term unemployed. This fraction has remained high since 1995 even though the total unemployment rate has declined. A similar situation prevails in a number of Western European countries (see, e.g.,

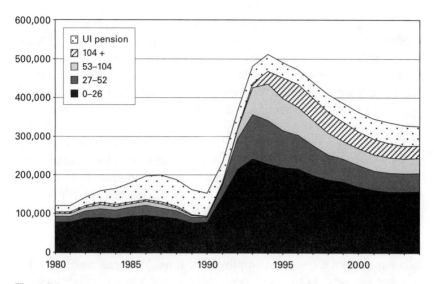

Figure 7.3
Unemployed by duration of elapsed unemployment. *Source: Finnish Labor Review* 2/2005

Machin and Manning 1999). The structure of Finnish unemployment is shown in figure 7.3, in which the unemployed are classified according to number of weeks unemployed ("UI pension" refers to the long-term unemployed who are over sixty and entitled to pension benefits).

7.1.1 Employment-Friendly Policies
Tackling the problem of long-term unemployment will be one of the most difficult policy challenges. An increasing fraction of the long-term unemployed are over fifty, and their return to employment tends to be difficult even when the economy is booming. Moreover, the incentives to search for employment are often minimal given that unemployment benefits are fairly generous compared to probable wage offers.

The Finnish unemployment benefit system has some special features that have a major impact on employment rates among the oldest age groups. Unemployment insurance benefits that replace on average 55 percent of preunemployment gross earnings are generally paid for a maximum of 500 days. In the early 1990s the unemployed who were over fifty-three when fired were eligible for extended benefits. These unemployed individuals could receive UI benefits up to age sixty and then could apply for an unemployment pension. Effectively, the extended UI benefits and consequent unemployment pension became an early-retirement system that made it possible to leave the workforce up to twelve years before the official retirement age. During the recession, firms made extensive use of the system as a "soft" means of reducing their workforce. As a result, entry rates into unemployment tripled for workers turning fifty-three, and very few older unemployed people found new jobs.

The policy regarding older unemployed individuals was tightened in 1997, when the lower age limit for extended unemployment benefits was raised by two years. Kyyrä and Wilke (2007) demonstrate that the policy change was quite effective. Employment rates for fifty-three- and fifty-four-year-olds, who were affected by the reform, rose to levels comparable with younger age groups. The age limit for extended benefits was raised again in 2005, to fifty-seven. This change is likely to lead to a substantial increase in employment rates for those who are fifty-five and fifty-six. At the same time, the unemployment pension system was abolished, but this was probably less important because now the unemployed can receive UI benefits up to old-age retirement.

Another important policy change that may affect long-term unemployment rates has to do with labor market support: a means-tested flat-rate benefit paid to those who have exhausted their right to UI benefits or who do not have sufficient employment history to qualify for UI benefits. As of 2006, those who have received labor market support for 500 days or who have received labor market support for 180 days after exhausting the UI benefit period enter a specific activation period. During the activation period these long-term recipients of labor market support are offered more intensive counseling and "activation measures" consisting of subsidized jobs and labor market training. According to the official target, the unemployed who do not find a job would participate in these activities for two years during a four-year activation period. It remains to be seen whether this policy will have the desired effects. Earlier reforms that tightened the benefit conditions for the young in 1996 and 1997 did not have a significant impact on employment (Hämäläinen 2006).

Tax policy has also been actively used to promote employment. Average marginal tax rates have decreased by about 6 percentage points from their peak in 1994. In addition, the earned-income tax allowance, first created in 1991, has gradually become more important. For 2006, taxpayers could deduct up to 3850 euros from their earned income before paying local income taxes. In addition, a similar but smaller deduction was introduced in state taxation in 2006. These deductions are phased out for higher incomes but still have a substantial effect on tax rates for middle-income workers. Since the deduction can only be taken on earned income, it provides an added incentive to enter the workforce.

In 2006 the government also introduced a reduction in employer contributions for firms employing low-wage workers over fifty-four years of age. The maximum reduction in employer contributions is 220 euros per month, and it lowers the payroll tax rate for a low-wage worker earning 1400 euros a month from approximately 21 percent of gross wage to about 5 percent. This reduction is phased out as earnings increase, so that it is reduced to zero when monthly earnings exceed 2000 euros.

7.2 The Aging of the Population

The second key challenge facing the Finnish economy is the antici-pated aging of the population. While many Western EU countries face the same problem, Finland is among the more extreme cases (see, e.g., OECD 2006). Figure 7.4 illustrates the current and projected

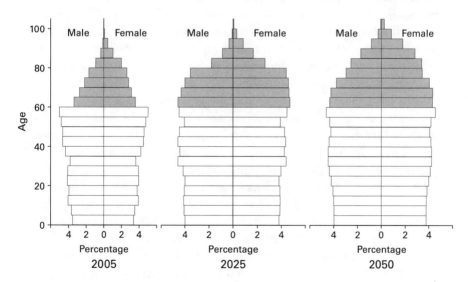

Figure 7.4
Population age profiles for Finland. *Source*: EEAG 2005

population-age profiles for Finland. The figure shows how the proportion of the older age cohorts will increase sharply in the coming decades. In fact, the increase in Finland will occur sooner than in most other EU countries because large age cohorts born after World War II will reach retirement age in about 2010. EEAG (2005) presents corresponding data for all EU countries.

The macroeconomic significance of population aging comes from its negative effect on economic growth. To illustrate this, we use the scenario in EEAG 2005. The current trend growth for EU-15 countries is on average around 2 percent. Assuming unchanged labor force participation and current forecasts for the increases in the ratio between pensioners and workers, the growth rate is expected to fall significantly in 2004–2050 to just above 1 percent. Per capita GDP growth will also be reduced because of aging, but by less than GDP growth. In the scenarios without aging, per capita GDP records a 2.44-fold increase by the year 2050, whereas with the expected aging the average living standards will increase only 1.64-fold. Thus, with the assumed productivity growth, the average living standard will still increase in absolute terms, but the demographic effect will reduce it by a third by 2050 as compared to the situation with fixed demographics.

The aging of the population leads to other economic concerns besides slower economic growth, such as pressures on public-sector financing. Attempts to counteract these problems must focus on increasing labor force participation, improved workforce training, and various other means of maintaining a high rate of growth in total factor productivity. Moreover, to maintain the core of the welfare society it is important to raise the effectiveness of public spending by improving public services via more efficient service provision.

Looking at Finland, the aging process is occurring against the backdrop of low employment rates for the age group between fifty-five and sixty-four. In 1999 the employment rate for fifty-five- to sixty-four-year-olds in Finland was slightly lower than the EU average and much lower than corresponding rates in the United Kingdom, the United States, and Sweden. However, the employment rates of age groups over fifty have been increasing recently. The employment rate of fifty- to fifty-four-year-olds is now 80 percent, close to the average employment rate for prime-age (thirty to forty-nine) workers. The employment rates for older age groups (over fifty-five) are substantially lower, but they have been increasing more rapidly than the average

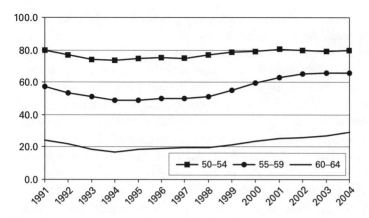

Figure 7.5
Employment rates by age group according to Labor Force Survey. *Source*: *Finnish Labor Review* 2/2005

employment rates for younger age groups (see figure 7.5). These changes are partly explained by policy changes such as increases in the age limits for entering various early-retirement schemes, by improvements in the education and health of younger cohorts as compared to older ones, and by the increase in the demand for labor after the mid-1990s.

As discussed above, the low employment rate in older age groups was in part created by the Finnish unemployment pension system, which pushed a fairly large number of people into early retirement during the crisis in the 1990s. The Finnish pension system[3] has presented yet other possibilities for early retirement. The disability pension has afforded the most common route. In the late 1990s, almost 30 percent of those between fifty-five and sixty-four received a disability pension. The individual early-retirement program also allowed those over sixty to qualify for a disability pension while meeting less stringent health criteria. This age limit was much lower during the 1990s— fifty-five until 1995 and fifty-eight until 2000—which at the time contributed to the large number of people taking early retirement.

These features generated a wide discrepancy between official and effective retirement age in Finland—one of the widest discrepancies in the OECD countries (e.g., see OECD 2003a). Finland undertook a major reform of its pension system at the beginning of 2005. The main elements of the reform process were increased prefunding of pensions, linking pensions more closely to life expectancy (especially increased longevity), and improving incentives to continue working. Finland introduced a scheme of flexible retirement ages (sixty-three to sixty-eight) with sharply rising pension accrual rates. Actuarial adjustments for early retirement were also increased and access to other early-retirement channels was restricted. Individual early-retirement and unemployment pensions were entirely abolished. These changes were partly compensated for by changes in the rules for disability pensions and unemployment insurance. Still, the most important change was probably a two-year increase in the lower age limit for receiving extended unemployment benefits.

The objectives of the pension-reform process are to increase the average retirement age by two years and to reduce the upward pressure on employer pension contributions for financing the pension system. It is too early to draw reliable conclusions about the success of the reform efforts. The changes will clearly increase incentives to remain in the workforce and are likely to increase participation rates. Restricting access to early-retirement programs will have a direct effect on employment rates. The question remains as to the likely magnitude of the effects.

Börsch-Supan (2005) and OECD (2006) conclude that the Finnish pension-reform initiatives represent a big step toward making the pension system more sustainable, but they express concern that strong incentives to retire early via loopholes related to unemployment and disability still exist. A further problem is that pension contributions are expected to increase substantially in spite of the reform efforts. For example, OECD (2006) predicts a 6-percentage-point increase in the contribution rate from private-sector wages by 2030. These increases partly stem from the long transition periods that prevent the reform initiatives from stabilizing the projected increases in contribution rates.

7.3 The Challenges of Globalization

In popular discussions globalization is seen as either a threat or an opportunity, depending on one's viewpoint. Once the depression years were over, Finland certainly exploited the new economic opportunities afforded by globalization, especially through expansion of ICT industries. Full membership in the EU in 1995 was a major milestone in this process, though the process of becoming an open and globalized economy has naturally involved much more than EU membership alone.

The threats of globalization arise from the need for structural adjustments due to new possibilities for the movement of capital and labor across borders and the possible outsourcing of production.[4] The mobility of capital for Finland was discussed in chapter 4, where it was noted that foreign direct investment flows, both out of and into Finland, have increased rapidly since the early 1990s. Finland has been a net exporter of capital during this period. The globalization of R&D has followed a similar pattern, because large Finnish firms (especially Nokia) have increasingly dispersed their R&D activities to different countries. The share of foreign R&D of total R&D by Finnish manufacturing firms more than doubled very quickly, from about 17 percent in 1997 to about 45 percent in 2001, after which the share of foreign R&D seems to have stabilized at about 40 percent in recent years (see Ali-Yrkkö and Palmberg 2006).

The international mobility of labor is another aspect of international factor movements between countries. A policy concern has been whether high taxes will make Finland less attractive for better educated workers. Pirttilä (2004) has assessed the factors behind Finnish emigration and immigration. Highly educated individuals seem to be five times more prone to emigrate than individuals with only a secondary education. However, thus far tax differences seem to have played only a minor role in migration choices. Emigration has not yet been directed toward countries with low tax rates. While emigration has increased, most emigrants have moved to other countries in Western Europe with nearly equally high tax rates.

As regards the outsourcing of production, systematic reliable data on outsourcing is not yet available. It is clear that outsourcing has gained in importance in Europe since the mid-1990s. Between 1995 and 2000, the proportion of total intermediate products represented by foreign intermediate products increased in Finland, as in most Western European countries. The outsourcing of production is one way of taking advantage of low labor costs in other countries. Within the EU, the outsourcing of production to the new Eastern European EU countries represents a real opportunity for many firms. Figure 7.6 gives an idea of the magnitude of the incentives for production relocation by comparing labor costs and productivity in EU countries for industrial workers.[5] The differences in terms of labor costs are relatively large and will probably play a major role in the future as regards location choices of both newly established firms and existing plants. While Finnish labor costs are roughly the same as the average in Western

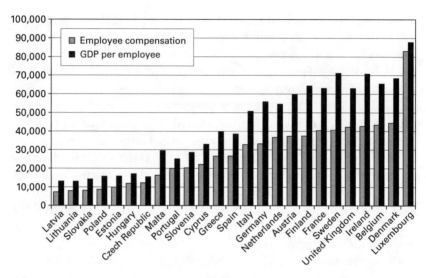

Figure 7.6
Labor costs in EU countries, 2000. *Source*: Eurostat

European EU countries, these costs are much higher than those of the new EU countries. Wage differences also reflect differences in productivity, and the latter are significant, as indicated by figure 7.6. Clearly, in outsourcing decisions firms must also consider whether they can raise the productivity of workers in a new host country through improved work practices and technologies.

The lower costs of inputs from Eastern Europe make Western European firms more competitive through outsourcing and at the same time the consumers benefit from lower prices. For labor markets, new problems emerge: in countries with highly regulated labor markets, including Finland, unskilled workers may find it hard to compete with workers in countries with low labor costs. Currently, this problem of lack of wage competitiveness predominantly affects unskilled workers, though more skilled professions may eventually face similar pressures.

International outsourcing generates both winners and losers. Beneficiaries of these new developments include firms engaging in outsourcing and offshoring of production, countries hosting the outsourced production activities, and consumers of the outsourced goods and services. On the other hand, unsuccessful firms and workers deprived of their jobs because of outsourced production are obvious losers in processes that redistribute production between countries.

It is important for governments to ensure that countries attempt to realize a net gain from globalization, although the policy responses to increased international factor mobility and outsourcing of production are not straightforward.[6] On the one hand, factor mobility and outsourcing are consequences of new economic opportunities and efficiency gains in production and contribute to improved global welfare. On the other hand, these changes pose challenges to national economic policies, which must foster adaptability to new modes of production activity and facilitate the movement of factors to new sectors from declining ones. Ways must be found to increase relative wage flexibility and improve worker mobility. This is a major challenge to the Finnish centralized system of wage bargaining, which has, on the plus side, helped to keep inflation relatively low but, on the negative side, has compressed relative wages. The latter development tends to reduce low-skilled employment (see OECD 2006, figure 4.6).

Preservation of sound public finances and of the welfare state is another major policy challenge in the presence of globalization and the consequent tax competition. In particular, tax competition has gradually led to lower taxes rates, especially in business taxation, though the trend is less clear-cut for personal taxation. These tendencies are putting pressure on public finances and the tax system, and relatively high structural unemployment and a rapidly aging population add to the pressures. These concerns pose a major challenge not only for Finland but for other Western European countries.

The future performance of high-tech industries is central to the resolution of these challenges. ICT has been and is likely to remain the key source for improved productivity in the Finnish economy.[7] Finland has had an excellent record in ICT, though a potential problem here is the focus on the production of ICT goods. As we pointed out in chapter 6, the role of ICT in Finland is markedly different from, say, that in the United States, where productivity improvement due to ICT has tended to involve the use of ICT in other production activities. It will be difficult for Finland to maintain a competitive edge in the production of ICT in the presence of technological convergence, new standards, and increased international relocation of production activities. Clearly, Finland must find new ways to make better use of ICT in other sectors, including the production of public goods and public services.[8] The latter would also help alleviate the pressures on public finances noted above. This would strengthen the economic situation of the public sector. Moreover, industrial policies should be geared toward more innovative use of ICT in other parts of the economy.

7.4 Epilogue

We have tried to characterize the Finnish economic developments over the last twenty years in order to provide recommendations for successful economic policies for other countries. It is time to recapitulate the main message of the book and to comment on policy responses to the current challenges facing the Finnish economy.

The Finnish case can be split into two dramatically different episodes. In the first episode, from the late 1980s until the mid-1990s, the Finnish economic experience has been summarized as a "tale of bad luck and bad policies" in Honkapohja and Koskela 1999. Major changes in the external environment arose from deregulation and liberalization of the financial system, goods markets, and other aspects of the economy. Finland had to respond to external pressures by opening up its economy to capital mobility and financial flows, and by lowering trade barriers. The liberalization process led first to overheating and subsequently to a crisis, which was a result of both negative external shocks and bad policies.

Though the crisis was partly the result of bad policies, it also initiated a process of major structural change and a redirection of policies that enabled the resumption of economic growth. Indeed, the Finnish story changed dramatically in the second episode, which began in the mid-1990s with the onset of robust economic growth. As discussed in chapter 3, the changes in macroeconomic policies were instrumental in overcoming the crisis. The policies were revamped at the end of the crisis so as to be supportive of the recovery and continued economic growth. In particular, membership in the European Union and subsequently in the euro area helped to initiate a program of macroeconomic stabilization, which supported the process of economic growth after the crisis.

The fast growth was fueled to a great extent by the emergence of the high-technology industry in Finland. As we have seen, the key prerequisites to a process of structural change favorable to a high-tech economy were largely in place and were not much affected by the crisis. The groundwork put in place both by the Finnish educational system and by the government's technology policy contributed to the success of Finnish industry. These were important characteristics, even though the business success of Nokia and other high-tech companies was the most important factor in the remarkable developments in the latter half of the 1990s.

Overall, the recovery of the Finnish economy from deep crisis is a remarkable achievement. The acute crisis led to a firm political commitment to overcome economic and social obstacles. This consensus in turn made it possible to adopt economic policies that helped to turn the crisis into the rapid growth that we have seen since the mid-1990s. No doubt, the severity of the crisis was crucial in achieving the required political will.

As discussed in this chapter, not all is well, and important challenges remain. Of these challenges, the slowdown of economic growth because of the aging of the population and because of pressures from globalization are likely to dominate economic policymaking for some time to come.

Attempts to counteract the slowdown in growth must be based on policies that mitigate the reduction in labor input, which is the main economic consequence of population aging. Further reform of the pension system may well be needed to provide strong incentives to older workers to remain in the workforce. Another area of reform concerns the young. In particular, the university system must be reformed, because university study times in Finland are among the longest in Europe (see, e.g., Jacobs and van der Ploeg 2006, figure 5).[9] Both of these reforms are aimed at offsetting the reduction in labor input that derives from population aging.

As regards globalization, its effects are still poorly understood. Though countries with high labor costs will lose low-skilled jobs and production to other countries, these tendencies will also affect the wage-bargaining practices. There is likely to be more flexibility in wage determination for less skilled workers. Labor market reforms should aim to improve the adaptability of the Finnish workforce to the structural changes likely to flow from the forces of globalization.

An important policy goal is the search for comparative advantages in a globalized world. As discussed above, future comparative advantages for Finland will probably remain in high-tech industries, particularly in ICT. A healthy ICT sector will require a well-trained workforce, of which a significant part must have university-level education. This again points to the importance of reforming the Finnish university system and shortening the educational period.

The problems gradually emerging from the current economic challenges are by nature very different from the acute crisis of the early 1990s. They represent a poorly visible, creeping crisis. While the crisis of the 1990s led to a determined political response, it is not yet evident that the Finnish political system will respond adequately to current and future policy concerns.

Finally, and importantly, we consider whether the lessons learned from the Finnish example are relevant for other countries undergoing structural change due to liberalization and deregulation.

The first major issue concerns the options for smoothing the relationship between deregulation and a boom-bust cycle. Our interpretation of the reasons behind the severe Finnish depression in the early 1990s, following the boom of the late 1980s, emphasized "bad luck and bad policies." The external shocks—that is, the collapse of trade with the former Soviet Union and the recession in the Western market economies—were exogenous and unavoidable from the standpoint of the Finnish economy. These external shocks played a significant role in the Finnish turn from boom to bust. However, the classic financial crisis in Finland was also fomented by poorly designed deregulation of the financial system without further domestic reform packages. Eliminating domestic interest-rate controls, allowing the private sector to borrow freely from abroad, and sticking to the fixed exchange rate even as interest-rate differentials between Finland and other countries became oversized all contributed to a strong lending boom at home and from abroad. This lending boom was exacerbated by an outmoded tax system that favored debt finance as well as by outmoded bank regulations. As a result, the private sector became financially highly vulnerable to changes in interest rates and in the exchange rate. Defense of the currency led to a tightening of monetary policy, with a resulting rise in domestic interest rates, and later to devaluation of the currency. This policy in effect placed a huge capital levy on that part of the private sector that had borrowed in foreign-currency terms. In brief, Finland did not couple the financial reform process with a package of appropriate micro- and macroeconomic policies.

Mitigation of the boom-bust cycle requires that financial market deregulation not be carried out in isolation. Both micro- and macroeconomic policy measures should accompany the financial deregulation process. A reform of the tax system and tightened bank supervision can mitigate the domestic and foreign lending booms that result from deregulation of the financial system and capital movements. Floating the currency is an important part of the macroeconomic-policy package, unless the country belongs to a monetary union. This should be an appropriate complement to financial market deregulation, because otherwise monetary policy becomes totally ineffective. Fiscal stabilization policy should also complement any financial liberalization phase, to reduce the amplitude of the boom-bust cycle. These policies were not implemented in Finland: during the boom, fiscal policy was expansionary, and during the depression, it was tightened somewhat despite the increase in unemployment. However, after the bust, improved monetary credibility—inflation targeting and a program of fiscal consolidation—played a role in the turnaround and resumption of economic growth in Finland that followed the depression.

A second lesson from the Finnish experience is that policymakers must continually facilitate the major structural changes made possible by the liberalization and deregulation of financial markets. The focus on structural policies is important even if economic policies succeed in mitigating the boom-bust cycle. The specific policies naturally depend on the structure of the economy, and the policy focus should be on the creation of opportunities for new industries and economic activities. In this way, appropriate policies facilitating structural change will contribute to robust economic growth.

The Finnish experience provides a positive example in terms of the second lesson. Finland's GDP growth per capita since the mid-1990s has been higher than in most OECD countries as a result of rapid growth in labor productivity. Earlier, growth was heavily concentrated in industries with high capital intensity, but during the 1990s attention shifted to rapid technical progress in the high-tech sector and to improvements in the quality of labor. Both of these changes boosted productivity growth and contributed to the great success of the high-tech industries. During the 1990s, Finland became a country with high R&D spending, and indeed the expansive structural changes were largely a result of the rapid ascent of the ICT industry.

Notes

Chapter 1

1. Cyprus and Malta joined the EMU at the beginning of 2008, and Slovakia will join in 2009.

2. Note that the indexes are normalized at 100 for the year 1985. Thus, the series cannot be used for comparisons of living standards—for example, to infer relative levels of PPP-adjusted GDP per capita.

3. See ECB 2006 for an assessment of these issues.

Chapter 2

1. The slow growth in Sweden since the mid-1970s has been subject to debate; see, for example, Gylfason et al. 1997 and Lindbeck 1997 and the references there for discussions of the faded Swedish miracle. While some studies emphasize that the institutions and policies arising in the 1960s and 1970s were vulnerable to domestic and international shocks as the main causes of slower growth, others emphasize policy mistakes that can never be entirely avoided.

2. In comparison to Sweden, it may be noted that Swedish unemployment showed a very gradual decline over most of the 1980s, which suggests that Sweden experienced less overheating in the second half of the decade. The GDP growth performance of Sweden supports this view; see Honkapohja and Koskela 1999 for the comparative data. A standard reference for the Swedish economic crisis is Lindbeck 1997. See also Calmfors 1996 and Jonung and Hagberg 2005.

3. Savings banks were the most aggressive competitors in the banking sector. Vihriälä (1997) presents some indirect evidence according to which moral hazard contributed to the expansive lending behavior of savings banks.

4. See, for example, Sachs, Tornell, and Velasco 1996, Corsetti, Pesenti, and Roubini 1999, and Radelet and Sachs 1998 for empirics, and Aghion, Bacchetta, and Banerjee 2000, 2001, 2004, Aghion and Banerjee 2005, Allen and Gale 1999, Allen 2001, Ranciere, Tornell, and Westermann 2008, Schneider and Tornell 2004, Tirole 2002, and Tornell and Westermann 2004 for theoretical analyses.

5. Comparing these developments to the Swedish situation, the two countries behaved similarly in many respects. Both rapid growth in bank lending and a huge rise in asset

prices also took place in Sweden after the deregulation. There is, however, one notable difference. The current account deficits were much smaller in Sweden than in Finland; see Honkapohja and Koskela 1999. This was important because it meant less pressure on the exchange rate in the case of Sweden.

6. See Honkapohja, Koskela, and Paunio 1993, section 4, or Nyberg and Vihriälä 1994 for a more precise description.

7. The share of foreign-currency loans in total bank lending was 13–15 percent in the mid-1980s and rose to over 27 percent by 1991, after which it again fell to low levels (e.g., to 6 percent in 1999).

8. Drees and Pazarbaşioğlu (1998) provide a detailed comparative discussion of the Nordic banking crises. A recent empirical study of fifty-three countries during 1980–1995 finds that (a poorly designed) financial liberalization increases the probability of a banking crisis; see Demirgüç-Kunt and Detragiache 1999.

9. The numbers for the postdepreciation years are naturally even higher since debt is measured in terms of the domestic currency.

10. Aghion and Banerjee (2005) also discuss empirical evidence on financial volatility and economic growth.

11. For an up-to-date survey of the recent theoretical and empirical literature, see chapter 7 in Walsh 2003.

12. Overviews are given in Cecchetti 1995, Hubbard 1995, and Bernanke, Gertler, and Gilchrist 1998.

13. The evidence on the credit crunch provided by Vihriälä (1997) and Pazarbaşioğlu (1997) is mixed. They see the decline of bank lending to be, at least to an extent, a result of weakness in loan demand. However, Pazarbaşioğlu's (1997) results suggest that banks' willingness to supply credit deteriorated during the banking crisis as a result of a reduction in asset quality, low profitability, and tightened capital requirements. Saarenheimo (1995) provided evidence of the importance of the credit crunch for investment in a vector autoregressive (VAR) framework, which extends the univariate autoregression to multiple time-series variables.

14. The empirical evidence on financial factors has been developed on the basis of microeconomic data from the United States; see, for example, Bernanke, Gertler, and Gilchrist 1996 and Oliner and Rudebusch 1996. These papers look at several different types of evidence on the broad credit channel of financial factors and monetary policy.

15. For earlier results, see Ali-Yrkkö 1998 as well as Honkapohja and Koskela 1999.

16. Bernanke, Gertler, and Gilchrist (1996, section 4) examine the differential responses of small and large firms in terms of sales, inventories and short-term debt, using financial reporting data from the United States.

Chapter 3

1. The policymakers attempted to achieve an "internal devaluation" via wage reductions before the 1991 devaluation, but it was rejected by the trade unions. As noted in section 3.4 the unions later accepted zero nominal wage increases for the deepest crisis years.

2. See also Giavazzi and Pagano 1990, 1996, which provide qualitatively similar empirical results using data from Denmark and Ireland for the 1980s and from Sweden for the 1990s.

3. Reports by the three foreign experts at the Bank of Finland also emphasize this and point out that there was no clear overall strategy for financial deregulation (see Bordes, Currie, and Söderström 1993).

Chapter 4

1. Clearly, regulatory impediments to product market competition have recently declined significantly for the group of EU-15 member countries, including Finland (see Conway, Janod, and Nicoletti 2005).

Chapter 5

1. The crucial assumption in calculating the growth in effective labor input using relative wages as weights is that firms operate under constant returns to scale in competitive input and product markets, and maximize profits by equating compensation with each worker's contribution to output. Even leaving aside the noncompetitive features of the capital markets until the 1980s, there are good reasons to doubt the competitive market assumption for the labor market. Hellerstein and Neumark (1998) found evidence of the differences between wages and marginal products.

Chapter 6

1. In principle, the concepts and of "high tech" and "New Economy" should refer generally to new forms of production that make use of advanced technological knowledge, including both information and communication technologies (ICT) and other new forms of production such as biotechnology. In practice, only the production and use of ICT is considered in the empirical analysis of high-tech industries, because there are measurement problems for biotechnology (see, e.g., the discussion at www.aeanet.org). The economic literature on the New Economy has grown rapidly and is quite diverse. Jones 2003 is a collection of review papers on different aspects of the New Economy. Dahlman, Routti, and Ylä-Anttila 2006 provides a detailed discussion of the knowledge economy in Finland.

2. Hermans and Kulvik 2006 and Hermans, Kulvik, and Nikinmaa 2007 contain a detailed analysis of the state of the biotechnology industry in Finland.

3. Multifactor productivity is broken down by estimating MFP growth in ICT production and in other areas of production and weighting those estimates according to the weights in direct output contributions.

4. See also table 8 in Jalava and Pohjola 2002.

5. The results are adapted from chapter 3 of EEAG 2006.

6. Ireland stands out, because its other sources of growth were higher than in Finland, Sweden, and the United Kingdom.

7. The table includes all the EU-15 countries except Belgium, Greece, and Luxembourg.

8. Pohjola 2002 presents similar data for the period 1992–1999.

9. See also Daveri 2003 for similar results. For another international comparison see, for example, figure 3 in Colecchia and Schreyer 2002. That paper shows that the contribution of ICT to output growth has been fairly high (above 0.5 percent per year) in the United States, Canada, Australia, and Finland. The contribution is lower (below 0.5 percent) in France, Germany, Italy, Japan, and the United Kingdom.

10. See the figures in Koski, Rouvinen, and Ylä-Anttila 2002, 57.

11. See OECD 2001b.

12. In somewhat older data, used in Daveri and Silva 2004, the performance of Finland seems closer to the EU-15 average.

13. See Rouvinen and Ylä-Anttila 2003, 2006, for more discussion.

14. See, for example, OECD 2004, 28, for the basic facts on Nokia.

15. The history of Nokia is given in an extensive three-volume book (Häikiö 2001), which is the basis of our description. There is also an English edition, published in 2002. An interesting, popularly written account of the earlier phases in the development of telecommunications at Nokia is Mäkinen 1995.

16. The P/E ratio is the ratio of the stock price to company earnings.

17. See Day et al. 2001 for a discussion of the organization of innovative activities at Nokia. As that paper shows, the Nokia experience demonstrates the importance of a flexible and adaptable organizational structure, suggesting among other things that new ventures do need their own space to develop.

Chapter 7

1. See, for example, Wildasin 2000 for a discussion of pressures on the tax system arising from increased factor mobility. Currently, in Western European countries including Finland, there seems to be a tendency to reduce both average labor taxes and the number of marginal tax rates on labor.

2. Honkapohja and Koskela (1999) developed a model of equilibrium unemployment using a framework of imperfect competition in product and labor markets (see, e.g., Layard, Nickell, and Jackman 1991). Computation of equilibrium unemployment for different periods suggested two important points. First, unemployment was below the equilibrium level as a result of the boom of the late 1980s. Second, actual unemployment rose above the equilibrium level, which also rose during the depression.

3. See Börsch-Supan 2005 and OECD 2006 for detailed discussions of the Finnish pension system and the recent reforms introduced.

4. For further discussions and references on outsourcing, see, for example, Bhagwati, Panagariya, and Srinivasan 2004; Feenstra and Hanson 2001; EEAG 2005, chapter 2; EEAG 2008, chapter 3; Kirkegaard 2005. The empirical literature on international outsourcing has grown recently and there is evidence that international outsourcing has had a large negative impact on the demand for unskilled labor, so that this type of outsourcing seems to explain the changing skill structure of labor demand. For instance, Hijzen,

Görg, and Hine (2005) have investigated the link between international outsourcing and the skill structure of labor demand in the United Kingdom. Moreover, empirical evidence from various countries supports the assumption that higher outsourcing will decrease wage formation of low-skilled workers and increase wage formation of high-skilled workers (see, e.g., Egger and Egger 2006 and Geishecker and Görg 2008).

5. Labor costs and productivity are measured per employee because of lack of data on annual hours for some countries.

6. See Kirkegaard 2005 for further discussion of possible European policy responses to outsourcing and offshoring. He emphasizes that Western Europe's policy response relates to the need to increase the flexibility of labor markets.

7. Hermans, Kulvik, and Nikinmaa (2007) suggest that biotechnology is unlikely to be a major source of growth for some decades into the future.

8. In market services labor productivity is close to the EU average and does not stand out in the contribution of ICT (see Inklaar, Timmer, and Van Ark 2008, table 5). Finnish productivity in the distributive trades seems uneven, with relatively low productivity in retail trade and high productivity in other areas of trade (see Timmer and Ypma 2006, tables 10–12).

9. In contrast, study times in Finnish vocational education do not seem excessive.

References

Acemoglu, D. 1996. A Microfoundation for Social Increasing Returns in Human Capital Accumulation. *Quarterly Journal of Economics*, 111, 779–804.

Agell, J., L. Berg, and P.-A. Edin. 1995. The Swedish Boom to Bust Cycle: Tax Reform, Consumption and Asset Structure. *Swedish Economic Policy Review*, 2, 271–314.

Aghion, P., P. Bacchetta, and A. Banerjee. 2000. A Simple Model of Monetary Policy and Currency Crises. *European Economic Review*, 44, 728–738.

Aghion, P., P. Bacchetta, and A. Banerjee. 2001. Currency Crises and Monetary Policy in an Economy with Credit Constraints. *European Economic Review*, 45, 1121–1150.

Aghion, P., P. Bacchetta, and A. Banerjee. 2004. A Corporate Balance-Sheet Approach to Currency Crises. *Journal of Economic Theory*, 119, 6–30.

Aghion, P., and A. Banerjee. 2005. *Volatility and Growth*. Oxford: Oxford University Press.

Ahtiala, P. 2006. Lessons from Finland's Depression of the 1990s: What Went Wrong in Financial Reform? *Journal of Policy Reform*, 9, 25–54.

Aiginger, K., and M. Falk. 2005. Explaining Differences in Economic Growth among OECD Countries. *Empirica*, 32, 19–43.

Alesina, A., and R. Perotti. 1995. Fiscal Adjustment: Fiscal Expansions and Adjustments in OECD Countries. *Economic Policy*, 21, 207–248.

Ali-Yrkkö, J. 1998. *Effects of Financial Factors on Investment Behavior by Industry—An Econometric Study Using Firm-Level Data*. (In Finnish.) ETLA, the Research Institute of the Finnish Economy, Discussion Paper No. 654. Helsinki: ETLA, November.

Ali-Yrkkö, J. 2001. *Nokia's Network—Gaining Competitiveness from Co-operation*. ETLA Working Paper, B Series, No. 174. Helsinki: ETLA.

Ali-Yrkkö, J. 2005. *Impact of Public R&D Financing on Employment*. ETLA Discussion Paper No. 980. Helsinki: ETLA.

Ali-Yrkkö, J., and R. Hermans. 2002. *Nokia in the Finnish Innovation System*. ETLA Discussion Paper No. 811. Helsinki: ETLA.

Ali-Yrkkö, J., and M. Maliranta. 2006. *Impact of R&D on Productivity—Firm-Level Evidence from Finland*. ETLA Discussion Paper No. 1031. Helsinki: ETLA.

Ali-Yrkkö, J., and C. Palmberg, eds. 2006. *Finland and the Globalization of Innovation*. ETLA Research Publication No. B218. Helsinki: ETLA.

Allen, F. 2001. Financial Structure and Financial Crisis. *International Review of Finance*, 2, 1–19.

Allen, F., and D. Gale. 1999. Bubbles, Crises and Policy. *Oxford Review of Economic Policy*, 15, 9–18.

Annenkov, A., and C. Madaschi. 2005. *Labour Productivity in the Nordic Countries: A Comparative Overview and Explanatory Factors 1980–2004*. European Central Bank, Occasional Paper No. 39. Frankfurt: European Central Bank.

Aulin-Ahmavaara, P. 2000. Työn Tuottavuus ja Työpanoksen Laatu. *Tuottavuuskatsaus* 2000Statistics Finland, National Accounts 2000, 26.

Bacchetta, P., and S. Gerlach. 1997. Consumption and Credit Constraints: International Evidence. *Journal of Monetary Economics*, 40, 207–238.

Barro, R. J., and X. Sala-i-Martin. 2004. *Economic Growth*. 2nd ed. Cambridge, MA: MIT Press.

Bayomi, T. 1993. Financial Deregulation and Household Saving. *Economic Journal*, 103, 1432–1443.

Bernanke, B. S., M. Gertler, and S. Gilchrist. 1996. The Financial Accelerator and the Flight to Quality. *Review of Economics and Statistics*, 78, 1–15.

Bernanke, B. S., M. Gertler, and S. Gilchrist. 1998. The Financial Accelerator in a Quantitative Business Cycle Framework. In J. B. Taylor and M. Woodford, eds., *Handbook of Macroeconomics*, vol. 1C, 1341–1393. Amsterdam: Elsevier.

Bhagwati, J., A. Panagariya, and T. N. Srinivasan. 2004. The Muddles over Outsourcing. *Journal of Economic Perspectives*, 18, 93–114.

Blanchard, O. 1993. Suggestions for a New Set of Fiscal Indicators. Mimeo.

Böckerman, P., and M. Maliranta. 2007. The Micro-Level Dynamics of Regional Productivity Growth: The Source of Divergence in Finland. *Regional Science and Urban Economics*, 37, 165–182.

Bond, S., J. A. Elston, J. Mairess, and B. Mulkay. 2003. Financial Factors and Investment in Belgium, France, Germany, and the United Kingdom: A Comparison Using Company Panel Data. *Review of Economics and Statistics*, 85, 153–165.

Bond, S., and C. Meghir. 1994. Dynamic Investment Models and the Firm's Financial Policy. *Review of Economic Studies*, 61, 197–222.

Bordes, C., D. Currie, and H. T. Söderström. 1993. *Three Assessments of Finland's Economic Crisis and Economic Policy*. Bank of Finland Publication D.9. Helsinki: Bank of Finland.

Börsch-Supan, A. 2005. *The 2005 Pension Reform in Finland*. Finnish Centre for Pensions, Working Papers, 2005:1. Helsinki: Finnish Centre for Pensions.

Calmfors, L. 1996. Nationalekonomernas Roll under det Senaste Decenniet—Vilka Är Lärdömarna? In L. Jonung, ed., *Ekonomernas Roll in Debatten—Gör de Någon Nytta?* Stockholm: Ekerlids Förlag.

Calmfors, L. 2001. Wages and Wage Bargaining Institutions in the EMU—A Survey of the Issues. *Empirica*, 28, 325–351.

Campbell, J. Y., and N. G. Mankiw. 1991. Consumption, Income and Interest Rates: Reinterpreting the Time Series Evidence. *NBER Macroeconomics Annual*, 185–245.

Carlstrom, C., and T. Fuerst. 1997. Agency Cost, Net Worth, and Business Fluctuations: A Computable General Equilibrium Analysis. *American Economic Review*, 88, 893–910.

Cecchetti, S. G. 1995. Distinguishing Theories of the Monetary Transmission Mechanism. *Federal Reserve Bank of St. Louis Review*, May/June, 83–97.

Colecchia, A., and P. Schreyer. 2002. ICT Investment and Economic Growth in the 1990s: Is the United States a Unique Case? *Review of Economic Dynamics*, 5, 408–442.

Conway, P., V. Janod, and G. Nicoletti. 2005. *Product Market Regulation in OECD Countries: 1998–2003*. OECD Economic Department Working Papers No. 419. Paris: OECD.

Corsetti, G., P. Pesenti, and N. Roubini. 1999. Paper Tigers: A Model of the Asian Crisis. *European Economic Review*, 43, 1211–1236.

Dahlman, C. J., J. Routti, and P. Ylä-Anttila, eds. 2006. *Finland as a Knowledge Economy: Elements of Success and Lessons Learned*. World Bank Institute Publication. Washington, DC: World Bank Institute.

Daveri, F. 2002. The New Economy in Europe 1992–2001. *Oxford Review of Economic Policy*, 18, 345–362.

Daveri, F. 2003. Information Technology and Productivity Growth across Countries and Sectors. In D. C. Jones, ed., *New Economy Handbook*, 101–120. San Diego: Elsevier and Academic Press.

Daveri, F., and O. Silva. 2004. Not Only Nokia: Lessons on the New Economy from Finland.. *Economic Policy*, 19, 117–163.

Day, J. D., P. Y. Mang, A. Richter, and J. Roberts. 2001. The Innovative Organization: Why New Ventures Need More Than a Room of Their Own. *McKinsey Quarterly*, 2, 21–31.

Demirgüç-Kunt, A., and E. Detragiache. 1999. Financial Liberalization and Financial Fragility. World Bank Policy Research Working Paper 1917, Washington, DC: World Bank, November.

Dornbush, R., L. Goldfajn, and R. O. Valdès. 1995. Currency Crises and Collapses. *Brookings Papers on Economic Activity*, 219–293.

Drees, B., and C. Pazarbaşioğlu. 1998. *The Nordic Banking Crises: Pitfalls in Financial Liberalization*. IMF Occasional Paper No. 161. Washington, DC: IMF.

ECB. 2006. *Macroeconomic and Financial Stability Challenges for Acceding and Candidate Countries*. European Central Bank Occasional Paper No. 48. Frankfurt: European Central Bank, July.

Edey, M., and K. Hviding. 1995. *An Assesment of Financial Reform in OECD Countries*. Economic Department Working Paper No. 154. Paris: OECD.

EEAG. 2005. *Report on the European Economy 2005*. Munich: European Economic Advisory Group at CESifo.

EEAG. 2006. *Report on the European Economy 2006*. Munich: European Economic Advisory Group at CESifo.

EEAG. 2008. *Report on the European Economy 2008*. Munich: European Economic Advisory Group at CESifo.

Egger, H., and P. Egger. 2006. International Outsourcing and the Productivity of Low-Skilled Labor in the EU. *Economic Inquiry*, 44, 98–108.

Elmeskov, J., and S. Scarpetta. 2000. New Sources of Economic Growth in Europe? Paper presented at Oesterreichische Nationalbank 28th Economics Conference, Vienna, June.

Fazzari, S. M., R. G. Hubbard, and B. C. Petersen. 1988. Financing Constraints and Corporate Investment. *Brookings Papers on Economic Activity*, 1988/1, 141–195.

Feenstra, R. C., and G. H. Hanson. 2001. Global Production Sharing and Rising Inequality: A Survey of Trade and Wages. *Handbook of International Economics*, vol. 4, forthcoming.

Finnish Economic Papers. 1996. Special Issue on the Crisis of the Finnish Economy, vol. 9, no. 1.

Flanagan, R. J. 1999. Macroeconomic Performance and Collective Bargaining: An International Perspective. *Journal of Economic Literature*, 37, 1150–1175.

Furman, J., J. E. Stiglitz, B. P. Bosworth, and S. Radelet. 1998. Economic Crises: Evidence and Insights from East Asia. *Brookings Papers on Economic Activity*, 1998/2, 1–135.

Geishecker, I., and H. Görg. 2008. Winners and Losers: A Micro-Level Analysis of International Outsourcing and Wages. *Canadian Journal of Economics*, 41, 243–270.

Gerlach, S., and F. Smets. 1999. Output Gaps and Monetary Policy in the EMU Area. *European Economic Review*, 43, 801–812.

Giavazzi, F., and M. Pagano. 1990. Can Severe Fiscal Contractions Be Expansionary? Tales of Two Small European Countries. In O. J. Blanchard and S. Fischer, eds., *NBER Macroeconomics Annual*, 75–122. Cambridge, MA: MIT Press.

Giavazzi, F., and M. Pagano. 1996. Non-Keynesian Effects of Fiscal Policy Changes: International Evidence and the Swedish Experience. *Swedish Economic Policy Review*, 3, 67–103.

Girardin, E., L. Sarno, and M. P. Taylor. 2000. Private Consumption Behaviour, Liquidity Constraints and Financial Deregulation in France: A Nonlinear Analysis. *Empirical Economics*, 25, 351–368.

Griffith, R., S. Redding, and J. van Reenen. 2004. Mapping the Two Faces of R&D: Productivity Growth in a Panel of OECD Countries. *Review of Economics and Statistics*, 86, 883–895.

Gylfason, T., T. Andersen, S. Honkapohja, A. J. Isachsen, and J. Williamson. 1997. *The Swedish Model under Stress*. Stockholm: SNS Förlag.

Häikiö, M. 2001. *Nokia OYJ:n Historia*. Helsinki: Edita. English ed.: *Nokia: The Inside Story*. New York: Financial Times Prentice Hall, 2002.

Haltiwanger, J., and R. Jarmin. 2003. A Statistical Portrait of the New Economy. In D. C. Jones, ed., *New Economy Handbook*, 3–24. San Diego: Elsevier and Academic Press.

Hämäläinen, U. 2006. Aktivoivatko Työmarkkinatuen Rajaukset? Kokemuksia Nuorten Työmarkkinatuen Rajoituksista (Do Restrictions on Labor Market Support Activate the Unemployed? Experiences from Limiting Benefit Eligibility for Youth). (In Finnish.) In K. Hämäläinen, H. Taimio, and R. Uusitalo, eds., *Työttömyys—Taloustieteellisiä Puheenvuoroja*. Helsinki: Edita.

Hellerstein, J. K., and D. Neumark. 1998. Wage Discrimination, Segregation, and Sex Differences in Wages and Productivity within and between Plants. *Industrial Relations*, 37, 232–260.

Hermans, R., and M. Kulvik, eds. 2006. *Sustainable Biotechnology Development*. ETLA Research Publication No. B217. Helsinki: ETLA.

Hermans, R., M. Kulvik, and H. Nikinmaa, eds. 2007. *Biotechnology as a Competitive Edge for the Finnish Forest Cluster*. ETLA Research Publication No. B227. Helsinki: ETLA.

Hermans, R., M. Kulvik, and P. Ylä-Anttila. 2005. International Mega-Trends and Growth Prospects of the Finnish Biotechnology Industry: Recent Economic Research and Policy Implications. *Journal of Commercial Biotechnology*, 11, 134–145.

Hijzen, A., H. Görg, and R. C. Hine. 2005. International Outsourcing and the Skill Structure of Labour Demand in the United Kingdom. *Economic Journal*, 115, 860–875.

Hodrick, R., and E. Prescott. 1997. Postwar U.S. Business Cycles: An Empirical Investigation. *Journal of Money, Credit and Banking*, 29, 1–16.

Honkapohja, S., and E. Koskela. 1999. The Economic Crisis of the 1990s in Finland. *Economic Policy*, 29, 401–436.

Honkapohja, S., E. Koskela, and J. Paunio. 1993. The Crisis of the Finnish Economy. In *Nya Villkor för Ekonomi och Politik*, SOU Utredningar, Bilagadel 2, 7–45. Stockholm: SOU.

Honkapohja, S., E. Koskela, and J. Paunio. 1996. The Depression of the 1990s in Finland: An Analytic View. *Finnish Economic Papers*, 9, 37–54.

Hubbard, R. G. 1995. Is There a "Credit Channel" for Monetary Policy? *Federal Reserve Bank of St. Louis Review*, May/June, 63–77.

Hubbard, R. G. 1998. Capital-Market Imperfections and Investment. *Journal of Economic Literature*, 36, 193–225.

Ilmakunnas, P., and M. Maliranta. 2000. Työpaikkojen ja Työntekijöiden Vaihtuvuus Laman ja Elpymisen Aikana. *Kansantaloudellinen aikakauskirja*, 2/2000.

Ilmakunnas, P., and M. Maliranta. 2005. Technology, Labour Characteristics and Wage-productivity Gaps. *Oxford Bulletin of Economics and Statistics*, 67, 623–645.

Inklaar, R., M. P. Timmer, and B. van Ark. 2008. Market Services Productivity across Europe and the US. *Economic Policy*, 53, 141–194.

Jacobs, B., and F. van der Ploeg. 2006. Guide to Reform of Higher Education: A European Perspective. *Economic Policy*, 47, 535–592.

Jalava, J., and M. Pohjola. 2002. Economic Growth in the New Economy: Evidence from Advanced Economies. *Information Economics and Policy*, 14, 189–210.

Jalava, J., and M. Pohjola. 2007. ICT as a Source of Output and Productivity Growth in Finland. *Telecommunications Policy*, 31, 463–472.

Jones, D. C., ed. 2003. *New Economy Handbook*. San Diego: Elsevier and Academic Press.

Jonung, L., and T. Hagberg. 2005. *How Costly Was the Crisis of the 1990s? A Comparative Analysis of the Deepest Crises in Finland and Sweden over the Last 130 Years*. European Commission Economic Papers, No. 224, March. Brussels: European Commission.

Jonung, L., L. Schuknecht, and M. Tujula. 2005. The Boom-Bust Cycle in Finland and Sweden 1984–1995 in an International Perspective. Mimeo, November.

Jonung, L., H. T. Söderström, and J. Stymne. 1996. Depression in the North—Boom and Bust in Sweden and Finland, 1985–93. *Finnish Economic Papers*, 9, 55–71.

Jorgenson, D. W., F. M. Gollop, and B. M. Fraumeni. 1987. *Productivity and U.S. Economic Growth*. Cambridge, MA: Harvard University Press.

Kalela, J., J. Kiander, U. Kivikuru, H. A. Loikkanen, and J. Simpura, eds. 2001. *Down from the Heavens, up from the Ashes*. Helsinki: Government Institute for Economic Research.

Kaplan, S. N., and L. Zingales. 1997. Do Investment-Cash Flow Sensitivities Provide Useful Measures of Financing Constraints? *Quarterly Journal of Economics*, 112, 169–215.

Kiander, J. 2005. The Evolution of the Finnish Model in the 1990s: From Depression to High-Tech Boom. In U. Becker and H. Schwartz, eds., *A Critical Comparison of the Dutch, Scandinavian, Swiss, Australian and Irish Cases versus Germany and the US*, 87–110. Amsterdam: Amsterdam University Press.

Kiander, J., and P. Vartia. 1996. The Great Depression of the 1990s in Finland. *Finnish Economic Papers*, 9, 72–88.

Kiander, J., and P. Vartia. 1998. The Depression of the 1990's in Finland: A Nordic Financial Crisis or a Result of the Collapse of the Soviet Union? In T. Myllyntaus, ed., *Economic Crises and Restructuring in History: Experiences of Small Countries*. St. Katharinen: Scripta Mercaturae Verlag.

Kirkegaard, J. F. 2005. *Outsourcing and Offshoring: Pushing the European Model over the Hill, Rather Than off the Cliff!* Working Paper No. 05-1. Washington, DC: Institute for International Economics.

Kiyotaki, N., and J. Moore. 1997. Credit Cycles. *Journal of Political Economy*, 105, 211–248.

Koskela, E., and R. Uusitalo. 2006. Un-Intended Convergence: How the Finnish Unemployment Reached the European Level. In M. Werding, ed., *Structural Unemployment in Western Europe: Reasons and Remedies*, 159–185. CESifo Seminar Series. Cambridge, MA: MIT Press.

Koski, H., P. Rouvinen, and P. Ylä-Anttila. 2002. *Tieto ja Talous, Mitä "Uudesta Taloudesta" Jäi* (Knowledge and the Economy: What Is Left of the "New Economy"?). (In Finnish.) Helsinki: Edita.

Kuttner, K. 1994. Estimating Potential Output as a Latent Variable. *Journal of Business and Economic Statistics*, 12, 361–368.

Kyyrä, T., and R. A. Wilke. 2007. Reduction in the Long-Term Unemployment of the Elderly: A Success Story from Finland. *Journal of the European Economic Association*, 5, 154–182.

Layard, R., S. Nickell, and R. Jackman. 1991. *Unemployment: The Macroeconomic Performance and the Labour Market*. Oxford: Oxford University Press.

Lindbeck, A. 1997. The Swedish Experiment. *Journal of Economic Literature*, 35, 1273–1319.

Machin, S., and A. Manning. 1999. The Causes and Consequences of Long Term Unemployment in Europe. In O. Ashenfelter and D. Card, eds., *Handbook of Labor Economics*, 3, 3085–3139.

Mäkinen, M. 1995. *Nokia Saga*. (In Finnish.) Jyväskylä: Gummerus.

Maliranta, M. 2003. *Micro Level Dynamics of Productivity Growth: An Empirical Analysis of the Great Leap in Finnish Manufacturing Productivity in 1975–2003*. ISBN 951. Helsinki: Helsinki School of Economics.

Mannio, P., E. Vaara, and P. Ylä-Anttila. 2003. Introduction. In P. Mannio, E. Vaara, and P. Ylä-Anttila, eds., *Our Path Abroad: Exploring Post-War Internationalization of Finnish Corporations*, 11–24. Helsinki: Taloustieto Oy.

Mayes, D. G., and M. Viren. 2002. Financial Conditions Indexes. *Economia Internazionale/International Economics*, 55, 521–550.

Mizen, P., and P. Vermeulen. 2005. *Corporate Investment and Cash Flow Sensitivity: What Drives the Relationship?* European Central Bank, Working Paper No. 485. Frankfurt: European Central Bank.

Muellbauer, J., and A. Murphy. 1993. *Income Expectations, Wealth and Demography in the Aggregate U.K. Consumption Function*. Oxford: Nuffield College.

Nyberg, P., and V. Vihriälä. 1994. *The Finnish Banking Crisis and Its Handling*. Bank of Finland Discussion Paper 4/94. Helsinki: Bank of Finland.

OECD. 2000a. *Economic Outlook*. Paris: OECD.

OECD. 2000b. *Literacy in the Information Age: Final Report of the International Adult Literacy Survey*. Paris: OECD.

OECD. 2001a. *Economic Outlook*. Paris: OECD.

OECD. 2001b. *2001 Communication Outlook*. Paris: OECD.

OECD. 2003a. *Aging and Employment Policies: Finland*. Paris: OECD.

OECD. 2003b. *The Sources of Economic Growth in OECD Countries*. Paris: OECD.

OECD. 2004. *Economic Surveys, Finland*. Vol. 2004/14, December. Paris: OECD.

OECD. 2006. *Economic Surveys, Finland*. Vol. 2006/5, May. Paris: OECD.

OECD. 2006. *Education at a Glance 2006: OECD Indicators—2006 Edition*, September, Paris: OECD.

Oliner, S. D., and G. D. Rudebusch. 1996. Is There a Broad Credit Channel for Monetary Policy? *Federal Reserve Bank of San Francisco Economic Review*, 3–13.

Ollila, J. 2000. *Building a Global Company*. Ehrnrooth Lectures. Helsinki: Hanken School of Economics.

Pajarinen, M., and P. Ylä-Anttila. 2001. *Maat Kilpailevat Investoinneista—Teknologia Vetää Sijoituksia Suomeen*. ETLA Research Publication No. B173. Helsinki: ETLA.

Pazarbaşioğlu, C. 1997. A Credit Crunch? Finland in the Aftermath of the Banking Crisis. *IMF Staff Papers*, 44, 315–327.

Perotti, R. 1999. Fiscal Policy in Good Times and Bad. *Quarterly Journal of* Economics, 114, 1399–1436.

Pirttilä, J. 2004. Is International Labour Mobility a Threat to the Welfare State? Evidence from Finland in the 1990s. *Finnish Economic Papers*, 17, 18–34.

Pohjola, M. 2002. The New Economy: Facts, Impacts and Policies. *Information Economics and Policy*, 14, 133–144.

Radelet, S., and J. Sachs. 1998. *The Onset of the East-Asian Financial Crisis*. NBER Working Paper No. 6680. Cambridge, MA: NBER.

Ranciere, R., A. Tornell, and F. Westermann. 2008. Systemic Crises and Growth. *Quarterly Journal of Economics*, 123, 359–406.

Rouvinen, P., and P. Ylä-Anttila. 2003. Case Study: Little Finland's Transformation to a Wireless Giant. In S. Dutta, B. Lanvin, and F. Paua, eds., *The Global Information Technology Report 2003–2004*, 87–108. New York: Oxford University Press.

Rouvinen, P., and P. Ylä-Anttila. 2006. Finland—A Prototypical Knowledge Economy? In S Dutta, A. De Meyer, A. Jain, and G. Richter, eds., *The Information Society in an Enlarged Europe*, 163–194. Berlin: Springer Verlag.

Saarenheimo, T. 1995. Credit Crunch Caused Investment Slump? Bank of Finland Discussion Paper No. 6/95. Helsinki: Bank of Finland.

Sachs, J., A. Tornell, and A. Velasco. 1996. Financial Crises in Emerging Markets: The Lessons from 1995. *Brookings Papers on Economic Activity*, 1996/1, 147–215.

Sandal, K. 2004. The Nordic Banking Crises in the Early 1990s—Resolution Methods and Fiscal Costs. In T. G. More, J. A. Solheim, and B. Vale, eds., *The Norwegian Banking Crisis*, 77–115. Norges Banks Skriftserie/Occasional Papers No. 33.

Schneider, M., and A. Tornell. 2004. Balance Sheet Effects, Bailout Guarantees and Financial Crises. *Review of Economic Studies*, 71, 883–913.

Staiger, D., and J. H. Stock. 1997. Instrumental Variables Regression with Weak Instruments. *Econometrica*, 65, 557–586.

Stiroh, K. J. 2004. Growth and Innovation in the New Economy. In D. C. Jones, ed., *The New Economy Handbook*, 723–751. Elsevier and Academic Press.

Timmer, M., and G. Ypma. 2006. Productivity Levels in Distributive Trades: A New ICOP Dataset for OECD Countries. Research Memorandum GD-83. Groningen: Groningen Growth and Development Centre, April.

Tirole, J. 2002. *Financial Crises, Liquidity and the International Monetary Systems*. Princeton, NJ: Princeton University Press.

Tornell, A., and F. Westermann. 2004. *The Positive Link between Financial Liberalization, Growth and Crises*. CESifo Working Paper No 1164, March. Munich: CESifo.

Uusitalo, R. 2004. Do Centralized Bargains Lead to Wage Moderation? Time-Series Evidence from Finland. In H. Piekkola and K. Snellman, eds., *Collective Bargaining and Wage Formation: Performance and Challenges*, 121–132. Heidelberg: Physica-Verlag.

van Ark, B., J. Melka, N. Mulder, M. Timmer, and G. Ypma. 2003. ICT Investments and Growth Accounts for the European Union 1980–2000. GGDC Research Memorandum DG-56. Groningen: Groningen Growth and Development Centre, March.

Velasco, A., and S. Chang. 1998. *The Asian Liquidity Crisis*. NBER Working Paper No. 6796. Cambridge, MA: NBER, November.

Vihriälä, V. 1997. *Banks and the Finnish Credit Cycle 1986–95*. Bank of Finland Studies E:7. Helsinki: Bank of Finland.

Walsh, C. E. 2003. *Monetary Theory and Policy*. 2nd ed. Cambridge, MA: MIT Press.

Whited, T. M. 1992. Debt, Liquidity Constraints, and Corporate Investment: Evidence from Panel Data. *Journal of Finance*, 47, 1425–1460.

Wilcox, J. A. 1989. Liquidity Constraints on Consumption: The Real Effects of "Real" Lending Policies. *Federal Reserve Bank of San Francisco Economic Review*, fall, 39–52.

Wildasin, D. 2000. Factor Mobility and Fiscal Policy in the EU: Policy Issues and Analytical Approaches. *Economic Policy*, 31, 338–378.

Zachariadis, M. 2006. R&D-Induced Growth in OECD? *Review of Development Economics*, 8, 423–439.

Zeldes, S. P. 1989. Consumption and Liquidity Constraints: An Empirical Investigation. *Journalof Political Economy*, 97, 305–346.

Index